GO CROSS

DEVOTIONAL

CARRIE PICKETT

Published in partnership between Andrew Wommack Ministries
and Harrison House Publishers

Woodland Park, CO 80862 - Shippensburg, PA 17257

ISBN 13 TP: 978-1-6675-0393-6

ISBN 13 eBook: 978-1-6675-0394-3

For Worldwide Distribution, Printed in the U.S.A.

1 2 3 4 5 6 7 8 / 27 26 25 24 23

Dedication

For God so loved the world that He gave His only begotten Son so that whosoever believes in Him should not perish but have everlasting life.

John 3:16

To all those who received the sacrifice of the Cross and to all those He loves who have yet to hear the Good News.

Contents

Foreword

The beauty of the Cross is the message that has and will continue to change the world. It is the love of God on full display so that we can truly see His nature and heart toward us.

What was a shameful death by the world's standards became the demonstrated power of God revealed to the world. On the Cross Jesus made a mockery of the devil's lies, sin, and death. Death lost its sting as Christ invited us to everlasting life through His sacrifice. No longer was the presence of God contained in a man-made temple, no longer was the symbolism of sacrifices necessary to appease God. Jesus fulfilled all the requirements of the law and ushered us into a new covenant relationship with God.

Distance, fear, and performance are no longer the covenant we are living in today. Because of the victory of the Cross, the grace of God has been shed abroad. The gospel message of redemption, forgiveness, and righteousness are now our everyday realities. Many have never truly learned or let the fullness of Christ's work on the Cross impact their reality. There is so much we can possess through His accomplishment on the Cross.

In this devotional, we are stepping into the daily journey of allowing Jesus' victory on the cross to become more than just a symbol of our faith.

Lord, show us in your Word the fullness of the inheritance we've received as children of God. Open the eyes of our hearts to truly understand the victory of the Cross in our lives today.

Carrie G. Pickett

DAY 1

The Demonstration of a Living God

And as Moses lifted up the serpent in the wilderness, even so must the Son of Man be lifted up.

John 3:14

The cross was the defining act of God's love because it ushered in a New Covenant relationship. What He has always had in mind for you is to show you the length, height, and depth of His love. The cross is not just a symbol of our faith, but it is the integral part of understanding what God has done for us. A death on a cross was such a cruel and shameful way to die. And the willingness of Christ to suffer such a horrific death being completely *innocent* was the power behind the cross. We understand that He took all our shame, all our sin—the very things that separated us from God...but God never wanted to be separated from us!

The cross is not just a symbol of our faith, but it is the integral part of understanding what God has done for us.

I am going to refer to 1 John 4:8-12 as a foundation for this devotional because it speaks of how God's love was made manifest to us (the cross); but I want to give a quick backdrop of how God foreshadowed a picture of His heart for us from the Old Testament.

God wanted to make the Israelites a people set apart from the other nations. People like the Egyptians, Amorites, Hittites, and Perizzites couldn't produce evidence of a *living* god. Instead, they had surrendered themselves to false gods and demonic philosophies. They worshipped man-made idols of these gods and made sacrifices to them.

At the time of their captivity, the Israelites were surrounded by the Egyptian culture and their gods. They were trying to stand in faith of the God of their forefathers, but they had no understanding of what it meant to have relationship with Him. He was their God, but they were wondering: *where is He?*

In Exodus chapter three, God comes to Moses and tells him that He sees the suffering of His people. He heard their cry and was going to deliver them. He also told Moses that he was His mouthpiece to Pharoah. God was going to give a living demonstration of who He was. Not only to Pharoah, but to the children of Israel. God was going to come with miraculous signs and wonders—an exhibition of might and power that no false god could ever deliver (Exodus 3:1-20, 4:1-9). You know the rest of the story: the pillars of cloud and fire, the inconceivable parting of the Red Sea, the giving of the Ten Commandments, and the golden calf the people demanded Aaron to make.

Even though the Israelites were freed, they became so surrounded by the "world's model" of ungodly practices that they forgot how to worship and relate to their own God. They still had Egypt inside of them and went back to what they knew. God revealed Himself then and in succeeding generations. He showed them how to be a different type of people in how they responded, how they acted, and how they worshipped and sacrificed. They were called to be set apart. There was significance in their obedience in how they carried out each letter of the Law.

Genesis 3:15 tells of the prophecy of Jesus and the cross: *And I will put enmity between you and the woman, and between your seed and her Seed. He shall bruise your head and you shall bruise His heel.* The serpent and the whole world were going to see something huge happen through this prophecy. God also spoke through the prophets throughout biblical history, and they prophesied about the coming Messiah. The children of Israel knew there was going to be a Deliverer, but their wait was in God's timing: *Where is our Messiah?*

The cross is what beautifully differentiates the Old from the New Covenant. It brought into fruition all of the things that had been prophesied. The Cross of Christ was God's original heart and desire for relationship. But unfortunately, the Law of Moses and the notion of relationship was overtaken and perpetuated by religious *gotta-do-gotta-serve-gotta-fear-gotta-earn-God's-favor-for-Him-to-love-and-accept-me* mindsets.

Many people don't know what relationship with God looks like. The whole goal of the cross was to bring man back into right standing with God; there was no more separation. We can now come directly to the Father and He readily accepts us because of the finished work of Christ! There is now no Jew nor Greek, no tradition, no cleansing rituals, no sacrifice that is required for atonement. Jesus *is* the once and forever sacrifice. The cross made the performance of rigid rules and the Law of no effect. The cross is where our victory lies.

At one point, the Israelites found themselves in the wilderness encountering poisonous snakes that were killing them. God told Moses to fashion a bronze serpent and put it on a pole. He was instructed to lift the pole up so that when the people looked at it after a snakebite, they would be healed. This was symbolic of Jesus and the cross; but why was a serpent on it? Jesus was crucifying the enemy. All the enemy's tactics, influence, and poison were reflected on that cross—crucified and rendered powerless!

Imagine that there are poisonous snakes somewhere in your house. Would there be an urgency about you? Yes! You would absolutely be looking to find out where those snakes came from. The same urgency should be applied to all the *snakes* in your life: destructive habits, fear, and the devil's lies. If you knew that looking to the cross was the answer for all those poisonous snakes, would you still try to see if there was another solution?

Jesus says the same to you today: *If you will look up, believe what has been accomplished for you, your sin and everything that separated you from Me is taken care of. I have redeemed you. You are mine!* It is an act of faith to look to the cross and take our eyes off the strife and defeat that screams for your attention. The cross is where your victory is. The power of sin and the devil no longer have authority within your life. That precious symbol of the cross represents all that Jesus did for you. When Jesus said it was finished, that is when your victory began!

Lord, today I settle in my heart that what You did on the cross provided everything I need. I see how familiarity and tradition have caused me to set aside truth. And for that I am truly repentant. I come boldly to You today and will draw from this study. Victory is mine and I refuse to let another day go by where I am tempted to believe the opposite.

I believe that this devotional will help you step out of so many difficulties because you're going to keep your eyes where they're supposed to be—not on the distractions of the world, but on the victory that is yours today. Can you briefly describe what you believe relationship with God means?

For further study:
Gen 3:14-15; Ex. 13, 16, 19, 20;
Mk. 7:13; Jn. 3:16; Gal. 3:28

As you go about your day today, ask the Lord to show you how much He loves you.

DAY 2

The Beauty of the Cross

Anyone who does not love does not know God, because God is love. In this the love of God was made manifest among us, that God sent his only Son into the world, so that we might live through him. In this is love, not that we have loved God but that he loved us and sent his Son to be the propitiation for our sins.

I John 4:8-10 ESV

When Jesus was talking to the disciples, He said, "If you've seen me, you've seen the Father" (John 14:8-9). When we learn more about Jesus, we get the clearest picture of the Father—His compassion, His mercy, His authority, His salvation, His righteousness, and more! This is who God is. When Jesus ministered to the people of His day, He confronted people who didn't understand

God's character. It is the same with us, isn't it? We confront all kinds of people who might think they know God and how He operates; but their lives reveal something different.

> God's love receives us in any condition, no matter where we are, what we've done, or how we see ourselves. His love is greater than our sin.

When we allow the world's way of thinking into our lives, that is what we'll follow. The Israelites and following generations in the Bible are prime examples. They couldn't see that a loving God was pursuing them all along. He wanted to be their one true God. But God's people blended with the cultures around them. Men took foreign wives and accepted their wives' foreign gods. They worshipped their idols and participated in their rituals. They made sacrifices of all kinds and even prostituted their women in the name of religion.

That is why God raised up so many prophets to communicate to the people: *Why would you worship something that has eyes but cannot see, and ears but cannot hear; a mouth but cannot speak?* God was trying to demonstrate that He was the living, holy God and help them understand that they were to be set apart so that He could dwell with them. That is why the Law came.

Why were all those requirements and instructions so strict? God was trying to differentiate the people of the world—their gods, idols, and sacrifices—from the children of Israel. The Israelites were to walk, live, and interact how God intended. In short, God's people were to worship and sacrifice with specificity because many of those things reflected and pointed to Jesus. As they followed the Law, their practices gave glimpses into the once-and-for-all *Sacrifice,* and confirmed to those who studied the Law the Messiah who was to come.

We are familiar with John 3:16: *For God so loved the world, that He gave His only begotten Son, that whosoever believes in Him should not perish, but have everlasting life.* It doesn't say "for God was so annoyed and irritated with the world...". Love is what compelled Him. It doesn't matter where you came from or what your background is. It is only when we believe in the completed work of the cross that we will not perish but have everlasting life.

Romans 5:6-8 further speaks of His love: *For when we were still without strength, in due time Christ died for the ungodly. For scarcely for a righteous man will one die; yet perhaps for a good man someone would even dare to die. But God demonstrates His own love toward us, in that while we were still sinners, Christ died for us.*

Many people misunderstand Jesus' sacrifice and how to receive salvation. They feel like they can't be truly saved until they first clean themselves up.

The following may sound silly but it will explain that idea. I had been training at length for a marathon but then it was canceled. I decided to begin CrossFit® to maintain my strength and endurance. This is an intense program and I had told my sister that I was going to begin that next Saturday. She asked why I just wouldn't begin the program immediately. I told her that I wanted to get into shape *first*. I thought I needed to do some push-ups and sit-ups so that I wouldn't look like a wimp or the weakest one in class. She laughed and asked, *"So, you're going to get into shape before you get into shape?"* Without thinking, I was going to *perform* a perfecting of sorts. I wanted to prep or *better* myself prior to what I was anticipating.

Then it hit me. This is what religion demands: *You have to get cleaned up; you need things in order before you can go to God for help.* Some think that His sacrifice first calls for a certain level of purity, justification, or religious standing. God's love receives us in any condition, no matter where we are, what we've done, or how we see ourselves. His love is greater than our sin.

If you were to meditate on First John 4:8-10 and hold these truths as the character and the revealed love of God, I believe that you'll fall in love with God all over again. God's love is not a one-verse kind of love. It's truly the heartbeat of everything that was accomplished on the cross—righteousness, forgiveness, power, ability, authority. You and I can walk in these things because they are the foundation where we find ourselves: *I know that I am loved of God!*

God is love (v. 8). This is the essence of who He is, the essence of His person. *Love was manifested toward us* (v. 9). Because of the cross, you can always look up and be reminded of how He sees you. *In this is love* (v. 10). Your love for God is not in how you serve, in how you pray, in how you fast. Religion will make you look at yourself. In Him we move and have our being. It's all about Him. Stop making this about you or you'll miss the beauty of the cross. Also, in verse ten: *He sent His Son to be the propitiation for our sins.* Jesus accepted the assignment and took your place. That could have been you dying and going to hell in your sin.

There are people who carry the attitude that they are loved of God, but fail to see the love God has for everyone, especially someone whose sin is looked upon as pure evil. I had a conversation with someone who had a difficult time believing the depth of God's love. He said, *"I think that it is wrong that this love message of God can really be extended to someone that has, let's say, abused a child. You're saying they can just come to God and receive salvation? I've never done anything like that. How can they have access to God like me? How do they get off that easily?"*

What I stressed to this individual was that God's love is so unlike man's definition; it has depth and width that it *can* cover all sin. This is where faith and belief come in. This person was coming from a religious mindset, so I turned the conversation around, *"Let's make this conversation about the enormity of God's love to cover all sin, but especially how the enemy doesn't want you to realize that. The enemy wants you to see limitations in God's character and nature that do not exist. Sin is sin, evil is evil; all have fallen short from God's point of view."*

We serve a living and loving God. He sacrificed His Son for the entire world—every tribe and nation. He died for every religious lie that has been perpetuated. The cross is the answer to all cultural problems and doctrinal differences! I'm telling you today, the analogies of the sacrifices found in the Old Testament—the sprinkling of blood from bulls and goats—pointed to Christ. But those recurring sacrifices just *covered* sins.

The blood of Jesus *washed* and *cleansed* us. His sacrifice never needs repeating. Our sins are forever removed. This is the power of the cross!

Lord, You are the way, the truth, and the life. You are my answer. I can tap into the Holy Spirit to help me discover the depths of Your saving love so I can share that truth with others. I only want the clearest picture of who You are and how You operate. Reveal more of Yourself to me today!

First John 4:9 says that God sent His Son that we might *live through* Him. How does this verse move you to live your life and share the good news of the cross with others? What part of your testimony reflects His forgiveness toward you?

For further study:
Ps. 115:5-6; Jn. 14:6; I Jn. 2:2; Rev. 1:5

As you go about your day today, ask the Lord to show you how much He loves you.

DAY 3

The Revealed Love of God

And you, being dead in your trespasses and the uncircumcision of your flesh, He has made alive together with Him, having forgiven you all trespasses, having wiped out the handwriting of requirements that was against us, which was contrary to us. And He has taken it out of the way, having nailed it to the cross.

Colossians 2:13-14

Did you ever play King of the Mountain as a kid? Sometimes it was not simply racing to the top. Other kids might have made it difficult as you ran uphill. They might have tugged at you, knocked you down, or made you lose your footing. For a kid, the greater the challenge, the more fun the game becomes.

As adults, though, the challenges to make it uphill in life aren't very fun. We trudge uphill to get to our purpose, reach a goal, or just try to make it through the day. In our spiritual lives, we may feel we are climbing the mountain of faith to get close to God. We may have even endured sermons that contributed to our climb: *You have to climb to that place of purpose; you have to reach a place of power. You've got to arrive at the position where God can do something with your life.*

The good news is that you have already made it to the top! God's eternal love for you was revealed through the cross. You can even say that your victory was atop Golgotha (the hill where the crucifixion took place). That is where your sins and your uphill battle died. You are not at the bottom. You may feel that people, situations, or sins push you down or make you trip and lose your footing. But that isn't the *truth*. The issues in your life have been forever settled at the cross.

> Early scholars of the Law studied the prophets but could only read of a coming Messiah. We now get to experience Him in real time!

When we look at the cross, we are not only reminded of the death and burial of Jesus, but we also marvel at His resurrection. He took all sin and separation to hell and left it there. As Jesus resurrected to new life, we too rise and carry resurrection life into our everyday lives. We can walk in victory, authority, and everything that Jesus died for us to inherit.

The uncircumcision of the flesh that we read in our opening verses refers to being a Gentile. Circumcision for the Jew was a sign of covenant relationship. But since Christ died to take away *all* sin from *all* mankind, we were forgiven and now there is nothing keeping us (Jew or Gentile) from a relationship with God. There isn't any accusatory voice that can make a charge against us! This is the revealed love of God: everything that could ever have kept us from Him was nailed to the cross. We have been made right with God.

Even though the Law was set in place for the Israelites, the Law was rendered *contrary* to man. That means man's flawed nature made it impossible to ever be perfect; therefore, no one would ever be able to fulfill the Law. Only Jesus could do what He did; only He could satisfy all the written requirements.

One of many prophecies of Jesus is in Isaiah 53:4-6. When you and I share the Gospel, we share God's heart by taking people to the cross, to verses that prove the truth of Jesus and how He fulfilled prophecy. We can tell them how He has taken our pain, how He has carried our sorrows. We can speak of the burden that was removed because He suffered for our transgressions and for our peace. By His stripes we are healed in our body, mind, and emotions. We share how we were all like sheep that had gone astray, but God's eternal love pursued us. He laid all the sin that separated us and put it on His Son, opening the door to relationship. Early scholars of the Law studied the prophets but could only read of a coming Messiah. We now get to experience Him in real time!

Hebrews 1:3-4 speaks of Jesus as the brightness of God's glory and the express image of God's person. Jesus upheld all things by the Word of God's power. When Jesus purged our sins, He sat down at the right hand of God. He became infinitely better than the angels and inherited a more excellent name than theirs.

Historically, kings would stand up and receive counsel from their advisors and then make declarations on matters regarding their kingdoms. But when the king sat down, whatever was declared was a done deal. When Jesus sat down at the right hand of God, He was declaring, *"I satisfied the Law. Father, Your will is completed. It is finished."* Our sin was forever taken care of!

No one could have been a more perfect sacrifice or fulfilled all prophecy to the letter. Our self-righteousness could never hold a candle to Jesus; we could never do anything that could have saved ourselves. Sometimes people only receive the salvation part—they only hold onto to the part that saves them from hell: *I once was a sinner, but now I'm saved. I once was lost, but now I'm found. I'll just figure out how to make it through life and struggle and just thank God that He was merciful enough to save a wretch like me.*

People try so hard to navigate life—to trudge uphill—by placing limitations on themselves and God. They take on the pressures of the people around them and don't seek God's help. They don't fully grasp all that Jesus accomplished for them and stay stuck in a religious mindset that makes them feel unworthy and not good enough.

Maybe you find yourself fearing that you've lost your salvation because you're ashamed of your sin. You are not greater than God. You cannot hold onto something that God has already forgiven you of. He forgave all! He didn't ask you to purge yourself of your own sin. He just asks you to acknowledge and confess them. Your salvation is a whole other level of freedom and hope.

The cross is a constant invitation to embrace Him and dwell with Him in perfect relationship.

Mistakes and bad decisions will happen. God doesn't want you to beat yourself up. Just turn to the Lord, thank Him for His awesome sacrifice. Run to the throne room of grace—meet Him at the *top of the hill*—and He will provide the help and encouragement you need today.

Lord, thank You for what You did for me. And because of what You did on the cross, I run boldly to Your throne of grace with a repentant heart and with a teachable attitude. I will endeavor to keep my eyes on who I am in the Spirit and who You are within me.

When we consider the cross, it cannot be something we rush through. There is more to be grasped, more of His love to be revealed. Have you recently spent time considering all that He has done for you? How can you make space for Him today?

For further study:
Is. 53:4-6; Heb. 1:3-4, 10:12

As you go about your day today, ask the Lord to show you how much He loves you.

DAY 4

Jesus Is a Finisher

And we know that the Son of God has come and has given us understanding, so that we may know him who is true; and we are in him who is true, in his Son Jesus Christ. He is the true God and eternal life.

I John 5:20 ESV

Why did God send Jesus into the world the way He did? Why didn't He have Jesus come with chariots, lightning, and smoke? There would've been an immediate, majestic appearance that would've caused the world to stop and bow.

I believe Jesus came as a man so that we could identify and relate to His humanity, to observe Him in the Gospels interacting in day-to-day activities. We see the boldness, compassion, love, forgiveness, and friendship of Jesus: *If you have seen Me, you have seen the Father.* God was showing man that relationship was what He was after all along.

This is the understanding that Jesus' life conveyed when we read I John 5:20: *that we may know Him who is true and that we are in Him.* God was restoring our identity. When we believe in His Son and what His Son did, we are no longer separated but joined together, alive with Him; redeemed from the power of sin and truly righteous. This is Good News!

In Matthew 27:51 we read: *Then behold, the veil of the temple was torn in two from top to bottom.* In the innermost area of the Temple was the Holy of Holies. Only the high priest could enter and make that one-time-a-year sacrifice for the people. All sins that were known and all sins that the people may have forgotten were to be atoned for. The high priest also prepared himself to be made *acceptable*, enabling him to come into God's presence to represent the people. This innermost area was separated by a very heavy and ornate curtain.

> We cannot pick and choose which scriptures we decide to live by, or throw out what others tell us isn't pertinent to the culture.

When Jesus took His last breath on the cross, the veil (curtain) of the Temple was torn. Now, we can't overlook this because this demonstrated something very significant. Being torn from top to bottom could only show that God Himself tore it, not man. God was releasing His presence by removing the barrier and inviting us into fellowship. Because of the blood of Jesus as the perfect and once-and-for-all sacrifice, we can enter God's presence totally cleansed, forgiven, and redeemed.

Had Jesus not shed His perfect blood and obliterated the power of sin, God couldn't have released His presence. If He had done so without the cross, no one would've been able to stand in the presence of a holy God. Every man, woman, and child would've been killed. Likewise, if the high priest in the Temple hadn't followed the ritual to the letter and the stain of sin remained on him, he too would've died in the Holy of Holies.

We are starting to see a complete picture of God's grace, provision, and desire for us. This is what I love about Jesus, He is a finisher. The cross was a demonstration of love, but it also showed that the Law was fulfilled in Christ, to include the prophecies of the Messiah that were foretold in the Old Testament. These were types and shadows of Jesus.

You may have heard some people talk about how the Old Testament isn't relevant. If there were no Old

Testament, how could we have understood the love of God, His true character, nature, and His promise of redemption? We cannot dismiss any part of the Bible. We cannot pick and choose which scriptures we decide to live by or what to throw out. The Word of God is His complete and authoritative voice for our lives.

We are not to add to the Bible either. So, when Jesus said the work of the cross was finished, it is finished. No one is bound by a set of rules and regulations. There is no reason for believers to ever feel disqualified because they haven't done certain things: *Well, you know, Jesus did take our sins, but I've been taught that if I fail to read my Bible daily, or pray in tongues, or if I don't this or I do that, then I have fallen short of God's grace.*

There is a new word for the Law and it is called performance. Performance says that you have to pray more, do more; you essentially have to be perfect. The enemy is crafty when it comes to performance. He will throw thoughts of inadequacy and people that will tell you that you need to come to a qualifying place before God. Your performance can do nothing to qualify you. Jesus qualifies you.

This is the Gospel message. Jesus settled our debt. When you have the Gospel inside of you, you will put an emphasis on prayer, you will want to read your Bible, and you will be led to serve. Not because *performance* says you have to, but it will be out of the abundant love and gratitude you have for Christ and what He did on the cross. The wellspring of life that comes from your relationship will prompt you to love others. The things you have been freely given, your heart will freely give.

We truly are blessed beyond measure! I'm telling you; the message of the cross is the revealed love of God. The enemy is trying to keep people from understanding how much God loves them. I have people all the time come up to me and say, *"Can you pray that I get a revelation of God's love?"* That is an amazing prayer to ask for, but you're not going to get it because I pray for it. I will agree with you with all the confidence that He will hear your heart. You receive a revelation of His love by understanding who He is, what He's done, and what He declares over your life. We go to the Word to see God's manifestation of His love for us—a heart-piercing revelation, not just a goosebump moment.

Our God has delivered us from the domain of darkness and transferred us to the Kingdom of His dear Son (Colossians 1:13). This is the love and grace shed abroad in our hearts. However, Ephesians 2:8 says that it is *by faith* that we can come to this saving grace, this great salvation. We do **not** all become Christians just because of what the cross provided mankind. People can receive the gift of salvation, or they can reject it. And if they reject it, when they die, they will go to hell. *Behold, now is the accepted time; behold, now is the day of salvation* (2 Corinthians 6:1). If you are not saved say this prayer in faith:

> *Lord, I believe what You did for me, and I receive what You did for me. I confess my sins and I receive Your righteousness. Thank You for saving me today.*

Many of you have already said a similar prayer. The Lord doesn't want anyone to perish; that should be the motivation of our hearts too. Who can you share this Good News with today? What specific things from your life will give witness to the faithfulness of God?

For further study:
Matt. 27:51; Eph. 2:1-22; Col. 1:13

As you go about your day today, ask the Lord to show you how much He loves you.

DAY 5

Our Perfect High Priest

But Christ came as High Priest of the good things to come, with the greater and more perfect tabernacle not made with hands, that is, not of this creation. Not with the blood of goats and calves, but by His own blood He entered the Most Holy Place once for all, having obtained eternal redemption.

Hebrews 9:11-12 NKJV

When we realize what God declared about Jesus in the *old* and see it fulfilled in the *new*, we can be confident with all the promises He declares in His Word. Why? Because we can know that when God declares a thing, He will bring it to completion. This is a powerful truth!

The Old Testament is a beautiful picture of God's initiative—His precise plan to bring us back into relationship. It was God Himself who took on humanity and came to earth as Jesus. He was human in every respect (Hebrews 2:17). He walked among men so that man could identify and relate to Him. His desire and love for man compelled Him to be the propitiation for all mankind.

When we speak of propitiation, we are talking atonement. Atonement is the reconciliation between God and humankind. Atonement is a combination of two words that mean *to bring into unity.* Jesus was the Son of God, but also the Son of Man. He alone could take our place, take all our sin, fulfill the Law, and bring us back into right relationship with Himself.

I want to highlight some key verses from Hebrews that reflect Jesus as our perfect High Priest. In our opening verse, we read about the Tabernacle of Moses and that it was made with human hands. A *more perfect tabernacle* depicts a heavenly one, far superior to the man-made tent or temple. And Jesus more than satisfied the office of high priest; He was *the* High Priest. He was the sinless and spotless Lamb making the sacrifice. Through His sacrifice, through this victory, there would be all *good things to come*. He didn't just cleanse us of our sin; it was much higher than that. Our High Priest wasn't just another high priest of the Tabernacle

> Sin has lost its power in your life, but it hasn't lost its temptation.

of Moses, or like the high priest of Solomon's Temple. This was God Himself!

When my kids were younger, they would play hide-and-go-seek. They would go in the center of a room, cover themselves with a blanket, and ask if I could see them. Seeing a *hidden* lump in the room, the answer was clear. Jesus didn't just temporarily cover sin in one big lump and leave it as an obvious fixture in your life. No. He completely removed it from your life so that it would no longer have power or authority. Death no longer had rights in your life. He removed sin as far as the east is from the west.

Those are the *good things* that verse eleven talks about, but there's more. You and I can walk in healing, prosperity, peace, and in the power of the Spirit. The fullness of the Kingdom is inside of us. God removed our sin and replaced it with His righteousness!

Not with the blood of animals but with His own blood did Jesus enter the Most Holy Place and obtain eternal redemption (v. 12). Unlike the high priests, our High Priest didn't have to perform sacrifice after sacrifice. He only had to do it one time. His love was that strong and He was without sin. Remember, the priests would have to purify themselves before they entered the Holy of Holies. If they themselves hadn't followed purifying rituals, their sin would've remained, and they would've died. The priest that entered this holy part of the tabernacle or temple had a rope tied to their ankle and bells at the bottom of their garments. If a ringing sound wasn't heard, that would signify the priest died in his sin and he would've been pulled out by the rope. That probably added stress and caused the people to wonder if any priest was "clean enough" to continue with the sacrifice. With Jesus, you never have to wonder. He was without sin.

For if the blood of bulls and goats...sanctifies for the purifying of the flesh, how much more shall the blood of Christ, who through the eternal Spirit offered Himself without spot to God, cleanse your conscience from dead works to serve God (vs. 13-14). This means that if the former was good enough, then how much more the blood of Christ? His blood purges and cleanses beyond the superficial and hits the conscience and the ill motives of the heart. It also breaks a *works* or religious mindset. This frees you to walk in a new creation reality. You move and have your being by what the Lord has done for you and how He now sees you.

And according to the Law almost all things are purified with blood, and without shedding of blood there is no remission (v. 22). Some things in the Law didn't have to be purified by blood, but most did. We see this in the Garden. When Adam and Eve sinned, God took the skin of animals with blood still on the skins and clothed them. God *sacrificed* animals; blood was shed.

He then would have had to suffer often since the foundation of the world; … He has appeared to put away sin by the sacrifice of Himself (v. 26). He put away sin. Where? In hell. You may think, "*Wait, I feel tempted every now and then.*" Sin has lost its power in your life, but it hasn't lost its temptation. That new creation reality is a true reality when you allow your born-again spirit to reign.

When you understand the power of the cross, it helps you realize that the power of sin no longer has a voice in your life. You will be emboldened to look at troubling or tempting situations and tell them they have no authority. Your emotions may be stirred but you exercise your dominion but shutting the voice of temptation.

I'm constantly teaching my kids to be aware of how the devil talks; and I am *training* them how to respond. The other day, my son Michael had a tummy ache. He had to be at an appointment but didn't feel like going.

I encouraged him to not give the enemy the opportunity to have a voice: *"Michael, let's step out in faith and go."* He said he would go but immediately added, *"But I know within ten minutes after getting there I will throw up."* I replied, *"Whoa! Did you just open the door to the devil and say, 'Come on in, in ten minutes?'"* He got the point and just smiled. He went to his appointment and was fine. He didn't have any more tummy issues and he didn't throw up.

We've covered a few of the *good things* we can experience now. One of those good things is abundance. Christ came so that we could have life in abundance (John 10:10). Weighing ourselves down with sin or inferior thoughts will find us living far below what Christ died for us to have. We have freely received, we've been redeemed, we're righteous. God initiated His plan because He loves you beyond measure. Let that fill you to abundance today!

Lord, thank You for being my High Priest. In Your perfection, You cleansed and removed all my sin once and for all. I am grateful that Your sacrifice allows me to live in abundance. Relationship, redemption, and right standing are mine! When I have You, I have everything. Allow me to see more glimpses of Your faithfulness in Your Word.

Does the truth of the *old* being fulfilled in the *new* strengthen your resolve and hope in God's faithfulness? Are there promises in the New Testament that are difficult for you to stand on? Why do you perceive these as challenges to your faith? Consider Proverbs 3:5-8 today.

For further study:
Heb. 2:17-18; Jn. 3:16, 10:10

As you go about your day today, ask the Lord to show you how much He loves you.

DAY 6

Reflection

In this week of devotionals, we have been rediscovering the heartbeat of the cross. God's pursuit of you was demonstrated in such a powerful way that it has (and will continue to) transform the world. This next week of devotionals will help the revelations we have covered sink deeper into your heart. Let the Holy Spirit quicken these truths to you!

The cross is not just a symbol of our faith, but it is the vital revelation to understanding what God has done for us. How have you understood the role of the cross in your life? What do you feel it says about your value?

God's love welcomes us no matter where we are, what we've done, or how we see ourselves. His love is greater than our sin. In receiving Christ, He lavished His love on you in a way that completely removed all the shame of our sins. How do you believe God sees your past sins? Are you still holding on to things that belong on the cross?

Sin has lost its power in your life, but it hasn't lost its temptation. Because of the cross sin has lost its power and given you authority over every temptation. How do you speak to temptation when it presents itself in your life?

DAY 7

Reflection

Early scholars of the law studied the prophets but could only read of a coming Messiah. We now get to experience Him in real time! We get the privilege to know the Messiah. In what ways do you pursue a living relationship with your Savior? In what ways would you like to see your relationship with God grow?

We cannot pick and choose which scriptures we decide to live by and which to throw out because they aren't pertinent to the culture. Relationship with Jesus means relationship with the living Word, both Old Testament and New Testament. How would you describe your understanding of the Word? How would you like to see yourself grow in your understanding?

DAY 8

Boldness Versus a Faith Crisis

...let us draw near with a true heart in full assurance of faith, having our hearts sprinkled from an evil conscience and our bodies washed with pure water.

Hebrews 10:22

The picture we have been seeing throughout this devotional is of a God who desired to restore relationship with mankind. Our Creator longed for fellowship with His greatest creation. I often hear people say how awesome it would have been to be in the Garden and walk side-by-side with God. Or to have been one of the twelve disciples listening to Jesus teach and watch Him work miracles: *Can you just imagine what that would've been like?*

Yes, you can! You can truly experience an abundant relationship because of the work of the cross. You can now go about your day walking in relationship with the Almighty God. This experience is just as close and just as tangible if we believe and abide.

> If you think your sin is too horribly wretched for God, that is pride.

We've talked about how Adam's sin caused a rift between man and his Creator. Sinful man could not be in the presence of a holy God. We've seen how the high priest would fall dead if his sin hadn't been purged before entering God's holy presence. In the Old Testament, man needed a high priest to go before him and present the sacrifice to cover his sins. It had to be the high priest according to the Law. The holiest place was not for just anyone. No one could ever do enough in their strength to stand before God.

Hebrews 10:19 speaks about this boldness: *Therefore, brethren, having boldness to enter the Holiest by the blood of Jesus.* This refers to the layout of the Tabernacle of Moses—the courtyard, the Holy place, and the Most Holy Place. In that Most Holy Place was where the Ark of the Covenant rested. That's where the presence of God was contained. We can enter the Holiest by what? The blood of Jesus. His blood has now allowed us to go boldly into the throne room of grace regardless of where we are. We can be at home, in our car, at work, and easily close our eyes and see ourselves in that Holiest place because we have been granted access.

Hebrews 10:20 says that *by a new and living way which He consecrated for us, through the veil, that is, His flesh.* The curtain or veil in the tabernacle was put in place to separate the common person from entering the place of His presence. The curtain was a symbol showing a barrier between man and God. When Jesus took His last breath on the cross and said, *"It is finished,"* that curtain was ripped from top to bottom. This *new and living way* was made possible by the rending of His flesh, the consecrating of His body. Jesus was wounded for all of mankind's transgressions. This opened the presence of God to us, restoring fellowship with Him.

Hebrews 10:22 tells us to *draw near with a true heart in full assurance of faith; to have our hearts sprinkled from an evil conscience and our bodies washed with pure water.* Because of the cross, you and I can draw near to God. Our relationship has been brought back to its original condition. You never have to wonder: *Am I good enough? Does God really love me? Am I really saved?* Can I say that those questions represent a faith crisis?

When you fully get a revelation of what was accomplished at the cross and you've received His finished work in your heart, you will have a true sense of freedom and assurance to boldly approach Him. When God looks at you, He's looking at Jesus the finisher, the one who completed the work of removing your sin. This is how you need to see yourself. This confident assurance is what is key.

Let me go again to Hebrews 10:12. I've shared this before but it bears repeating: *But this Man, after He had offered one sacrifice for sins forever, sat down at the right hand of God.* This sacrifice was a "one and done." This is God's all-encompassing love for man. This illustrates how God craved to have fellowship restored. If you think your sin is too horribly wretched for God, that is pride. I love you enough to tell you that you are giving voice and authority to that sin and allowing it to separate you from God's presence.

If you are a born-again believer and still wrestle with this kind of thinking, know it's the enemy trying to keep you separated and to keep you from running boldly to the throne of grace. Hebrews 10:14 says: *For by one offering He has perfected forever those who are being sanctified.* This is what happened in your spirit when you accepted Christ. He has forever perfected the spirit part of you. You have Christ Himself living inside of your spirit. When you die and shed your earthly, mortal body and stand before the King, you'll stand in perfect righteousness. As we live, we are being sanctified. That means as we listen to the Spirit within, we gain a revelation of who we are. We are not those who give place to the devil, but instead dive into the Word; we are being sanctified, transformed, and set apart by the renewing of our minds (Romans 12:2).

We start to realize: *This sin has no authority over me!* We stand in a bold assurance of what Jesus accomplished, and out of our Spirit, we release truth to our hearts, minds, emotions. We don't have a faith crisis or waver in our decisions, reactions, or opportunities.

The beautiful side of this renewal is that the people around you get to experience this powerful revelation as it impacts how we speak, how we live. This is the victory we have in the cross!

Lord, I am drawing near to You today. Regardless of what I am facing today, I can walk with full competence and assurance in Your love for me. You are able to give me wisdom and physical stamina no matter what the enemy has been trying to drag me through. I thank You for Your presence, Your provision, and the position I have in You!

We get to choose how close our relationship with God can be. We can have the full assurance that He has an *open-door policy* for our lives. If you feel you are experiencing a crisis of faith, what will you bring to Him today? He promises direction and clarity to everything you bring to Him.

For further study:
Tit. 3:4-7; Heb. 4:12, 14; Rom. 12:2

As you go about your day today, ask the Lord to show you how much He loves you.

DAY 9

We Are the Temple of God

I will greatly rejoice in the LORD; my soul shall exult in my God, for he has clothed me with the garments of salvation; he has covered me with the robe of righteousness, as a bridegroom decks himself like a priest with a beautiful headdress, and as a bride adorns herself with her jewels.

Isaiah 61:10 ESV

This verse is so amazingly beautiful because it depicts a covenant relationship. We don't lavish a stranger with our prized possessions, do we? What He has for us belongs to us because we belong to Him. Jesus, in His position as High Priest, being both Son of God and Son of Man, was the only one who could take away the sin of the world. He was our spotless sacrificial Lamb; this was God Himself. This is the centerpiece of the Gospel!

The purpose of the cross was not only about restoring the relationship; and it didn't just fulfill the Law to bring the Old Covenant to completion. God's other purpose was for us to be the New Covenant Tabernacle.

> Because of His death and resurrection, the eternal Jesus is the one standing before God and lives to make intercession for us. His priesthood is without end.

But now He has obtained a more excellent ministry, inasmuch as He is also Mediator of a better covenant, which was established on better promises (Hebrews 8:6). He guarantees a better covenant with God (Hebrews 7:22). A better ministry is the New Covenant relationship. There would be no need for repeated sacrifice. Jesus was (and is) the Mediator, or the one who intervened, and took all the requirements of old. He forgave and removed sin completely. He suffered so that we would now have access to His promises.

Also, there were many priests, because they were prevented by death from continuing (Hebrews 7:23). There were many who served in the office of the high priest from the time of the Law to the time of Jesus. And because every man is subject to die, there had to be succeeding priests to fulfill the law. Death obviously interrupted a high priest's duties.

But He, because He continues forever, has an unchangeable priesthood (v. 24). Because of His death and resurrection, Jesus is the one standing before God and lives to make intercession for us (v. 25). His priesthood is without end.

The Law, the priests, the layout of the tabernacle and temple, all defined the way man could get their sins covered. Sin was never completely removed, nor could man come into a better covenant until Jesus. The Most Holy Place and the Holy of Holies were types and shadows that pointed to where God's presence would eventually land. His presence now dwells within the believer.

Being filled with the presence of God means you and I have become the tabernacle. This is important because God knew that we would still encounter an enemy on a mission. The devil is going to constantly tell you how weak and inferior you are. He will tell you to compare yourself with others so that you judge yourself as one without gifts or talents.

When you get the revelation that you are now the temple of the living God, you become bad news to the devil. You have the boldness to say, *"I may be in this world, but I am not of it. Who do you think you are, devil? Let me tell you exactly who God makes His dwelling place with...me!"* The enemy is terrified of you taking hold of this revelation because it means you're going to live in the inheritance of Kingdom blessings *and* with the glory of the Lord shining through you.

Your vestments of victory are the garments of salvation and robes of righteousness. He says, *"I want you to wear and walk in your victory so that you will be a living testimony of what Christ did for you."* I think the picture in Isaiah 61:10 powerfully illustrates the glory you are now clothed with, just like Adam was clothed before the fall. You are to arise and shine for the glory of the Lord is upon you (Isaiah 60:1). You shine before man and the enemy.

Even though the devil is on a mission, we can rest and know that our Savior is at the right hand of God making intercession for us (Romans 8:34). The enemy will always try to get us to be self-absorbed and self-focused. But when we take our eyes off ourselves and look at the cross, we will start to operate as the new creatures God destined us to be: *Therefore, if anyone is in Christ, he is a new creation; old things have passed away; behold, all things have become new* (II Corinthians 5:17). The word behold means to stop, consider, look upon, meditate. Let the truth of this verse settle in your heart and set your sights on your new creation reality. Allow the complete work of the cross and your position in Christ operate to overflowing.

Temples of the Holy Spirit are not supposed to look or sound like the rest of the world. The goal of the cross was to call us to a whole other level where you and I don't get easily entangled, enslaved, or distracted by what is happening around us. When we can truly take hold of *Who* we host, we can walk around with a boldness of our victory no matter what challenges of everyday life, people, or situations try to bombard us with. We'll face things head on from a place of victory. Nothing can stand against the Holy of Holies, the King of kings, or the Lord of lords that lives on the inside of us!

Lord, there is this confidence and full assurance that I need to be walking in; and that only comes when I truly consider all that You have accomplished. I praise You for constantly making intercession for me. Help me to draw near to You and to see You as my deepest desire. Help me to see myself clothed with Your glory.

How is your covenant relationship with the Lord today? Most people don't necessarily walk thinking that they host the living God inside of them. If they had, we would see more demonstrations of His goodness, His power, and His peace. What can you take from this lesson today that will help you get to a place where you are not moved by people, situations, or the world's voice?

For further study:
Is. 60:1; Rom. 8:9-11

As you go about your day today, ask the Lord to show you how much He loves you.

DAY 10

The Grace To Live Differently

Or do you not know that your body is a temple of the Holy Spirit within you, whom you have from God? You are not your own.

I Corinthians 6:19 ESV

Here's a truth that can change your whole world. Not only can it change *your* whole world, but it can also change *the* world.

As we grow in the knowledge that we are the temples of the Holy Spirit, we transform into available vessels surrendered to the reality of God's power within us. We begin to make movement toward others as God's hands and feet. Our mouths give voice to the authority of His Word to a watching world. People will wonder what is different about us. It is no longer we who live, but it's Christ that lives within us (Galatians 2:20).

Understanding that we have God Almighty within us strengthens our resolve to carry out what God has destined for us.

We have the living God inside of us and are called to walk in that reality!

Additionally, when we link arms with other believers who have a revelation of *Who* dwells within them, there is tremendous unity. Our anointings and giftings will vary, but together we can manifest the fullness of God as the Body of Christ. *Behold, how good and how pleasant it is when brothers dwell in unity* (Psalm 133:1)! Unity has the potential for the resurrection power of God to be revealed in our lives, ministries, and churches. Unity is a threat to the enemy because our influence can greatly impact the destiny of someone else.

When we said *yes* to Jesus, we were given grace to be different. This is why the Apostle Paul admonished believers to put off your old selves, which grows *corrupt through deceitful desires, and to be renewed in the spirit of your mind* (Ephesians 4:22-23 ESV). While we have God within us, we still have a free will, and if we don't renew our minds to what the cross has provided, we set ourselves up to follow our former conduct—to give into the flesh or to chase the traditions of the world.

The goal of the cross was to be life-giving, enabling us to see our true selves in the Spirit: *I am not who I used to be, and my desire is not for the world. My victory lies in what Jesus did for me; so, I am empowered to deny my flesh.* However, many of you may think that you'll never be free from the pull of addiction, from emotional outbursts, or depression. You've tried to *do* better but then fell short. You have been trapped in the enemy's lies for so long that old patterns have become your accepted norm.

You can put off those things! Paul encouraged believers to *put on the new self, created after the likeness of God in true righteousness and holiness* (Ephesians 4:24 ESV). This is similar to what we covered yesterday about being clothed in the garment of salvation and wearing the robe of righteousness (Isaiah 61:10). Seeing yourself clothed with righteousness and holiness is a mentality—it's part of mind renewal. Living in true righteousness and holiness is never according to a religious mindset but according to God!

When you put on the new man, you can reflect the image of God. Paul was reminding believers they weren't to behave like idolators living in deception. This is not what they were called to: *Do you not know that you're a temple of God, and that the Spirit of God dwells within you*? We are given the same reminder today.

Our salvation experience was not just for eternal life. Yes, we are heaven-bound but that shouldn't give license to live how we want to, when we want to, and "skate" into heaven. We have the living God inside of us and are called to walk in that reality! Each day offers opportunities to discover the fullness of what relationship with Him produces in our lives—how and when it is to be released, and to whom.

If we could demonstrate *all* the potential of the inheritance that is within us, it would take multiple lifetimes. But we only have one life to live and are destined for this time and for our individual assignments. As we release *His* life, we will start to see people and situations changed by the power of the cross.

The cross reveals God's love, but it also shows us that we were bought at price—purchased by the precious blood of Jesus. *Therefore, glorify God in your body and in your spirit, which are God's* (I Corinthians 6:20). God saw you are worthy; you have tremendous value!

Now, I have heard that verse "preached up" from a religious perspective, where value wasn't the key emphasis, but rather a list of condemning *"don't dos."*

This had the tendency to turn the people toward a self-condemning, religious mindset because there were not "measuring up."

First Corinthians 6:20 was written with the love of God. He saw you as precious and valuable. He still sees you that way! You were worthy to be bought at such a high cost. So, it is now out of a grateful heart and love for what God has done for you that you willingly choose to glorify God in your body and spirit. This is the lifestyle we are called to. We are being sanctified and renewed when we give place to the Spirit and allow Him to speak and direct our lives. We are to be different.

Be encouraged today. When God sees you, He sees that resurrected, almighty King of kings, defeater of sin, hell, and the grave living inside of you. When you stand in your authority, you create space to release Kingdom potential—for vision, strategy, and transformation. He sees your incredible value today and says to you, "*You are the very one I want to live in!*"

Lord, my life belongs to You. I surrender my life to You. My life is not my own. My purpose is not about me and what I want, where I want it, and how I want it. I want to live in Your timelines and the opportunities You place before me. I am grateful for how You value me. Help me to fully grasp the Kingdom potential that lives within me.

The Spirit of God calls us to get past the limited vision we tend to have for ourselves. What can come against you? The very things we don't understand surely can come against us. Will you carve out time for Him and truly seek His heart for understanding? You've been given the grace to live differently. Maybe it's also a call to approach Him differently? To expect from Him differently? What is He speaking to your heart?

For further study:
Ps. 133:1; Rom. 12:1-2;
Gal. 2:20; Eph. 4:22-24

As you go about your day today, ask the Lord to show you how much He loves you.

DAY 11

Positioned in Relationship

...looking unto Jesus, the author and finisher of our faith, who for the joy that was set before Him endured the cross, despising the shame, and has sat down at the right hand of the throne of God.

Hebrews 12:2

Every revelation of God's love for you has its starting point at the cross. We have been going line by line to see God's redemptive story unfold and then reach its climatic fulfillment in Christ. The cross is always the basis for God's love. No matter what we think about ourselves, no matter what anyone else has spoken over our lives, the cross settles any doubt and every question: *Christ proved God's passionate love for us by dying in our place while we were still lost and ungodly!* When you understand what the cross accomplished, you then start to walk in the victory and authority of Christ in you, the hope of glory!

In addition to prophecies fulfilled and the end of the Law, the cross positions us in righteousness. In Christ dwells all the fullness of the Godhead bodily (Colossians 2:9); and by virtue of the cross, we become the temple of the Holy Spirit. These were indeed the goals of the cross God had in mind; but I want to put emphasis on the position of our restored relationship. We were created for this relationship. We saw the depiction of God releasing Himself toward man when the temple curtain was torn, inviting us into fellowship. No longer was there a barrier. The Creator wanted to restore fellowship with His creation.

I believe that an intimate relationship with a holy God is the most powerful position we could ever find ourselves in. We have a fellow heir, Christ Jesus ruling and reigning in our hearts; and a teacher and guide in the Holy Spirit—one who will never leave or forsake us. Truly, this is a union beyond compare.

I used Hebrews 12:2 as my opening verse because it gets to the heart of what I want to highlight regarding relationship. Jesus is the author and finisher of our faith. Only He was without sin and obedient to fulfill the will of the Father. But pay attention to the words, *for the joy that was set before Him*. When Jesus was on the cross, He was filled with joy, He had vision. Though He suffered a brutal and cruel death, He endured the cross. A death on the cross was the most shameful way to die at that time, reserved for only the worst criminals, the most ungodly. But this shameful death was not about Him. It didn't matter the public humiliation that came upon Him, or the contempt others felt toward Him. Can you imagine the devil whispering before He was led like a lamb to the slaughter: *"Shame? Really? You want this dishonor attached to your name forever? Surely, there is another way to prove yourself to these miserable souls. Hear them yell, 'Crucify! Crucify!' What worth are they?"*

The cross was not about Him; it was about us.

Jesus was on that cross, but He was looking ahead. He envisioned a future where you and I would be in a close relationship with Him. The cross was not about Him; it was about us. He wanted to settle sin and death once and for all. While He bled and was mocked by onlookers, *we were the joy that was set before Him*. He despised the shame. This was His redemption story. This is the revealed love of God.

Have you struggled with shame or felt like you couldn't make any solid decisions? Trust that the cross brought you into a whole other level of freedom that enables you to crush shame, guilt, and condemnation. We all have made unwise choices, but you can be like Jesus and despise the shame and everything attached to it. Set your sights on your intimate relationship with God. That is your joy. He can touch and redeem any shame from your past, but you have to bring it to Him. He turns things around for your good.

In First John 5:1, it reads: *Whoever believes that Jesus is the Christ is born of God, and everyone who loves Him who begot also loves Him who is begotten of Him.* This verse is basically saying that your place of unity begins when you freely choose to believe in the Son. The fact that we can choose is a demonstration of His love alone. He will not violate free will.

More importantly, this verse is also saying that if we believe, we can become the sons of God. We don't work to earn that position or labor to maintain it. We just simply believe and come into a position of inheritance and royalty. The enemy hates this. Had he known of the *good things to come*, he never would have used people to plot against Jesus.

God knew what this redemptive story was going to accomplish. That's why there was joy at the cross. He had you in mind all along. You may think: *I don't even like myself; what could God possibly see?* The truth is that the enemy has been lying to you for a long time. God placed value on you, and because of that value and His vision of you, He suffered an agonizing death. You were truly worth that much to Him.

John 1:12-13 reads: *But as many as received Him, to them He gave the right to become children of God, to those who believe in His name: who were born, not of blood, nor of the will of the flesh, nor of the will of man, but of God.* You are not a mistake. You're not just some random occurrence. The vision of the cross was to bring you into that position of sonship. When you're confident as a son, you'll run to your intimate relationship with Him, and you'll respond to Him as your true Father—one that never leaves or forsakes you.

When you share the Gospel with someone, you share the redemptive story of the cross. You tell of what Jesus did—He took their sin and shame. He died in their place. You arc inviting them into a family. You emphasize that the finished work of the cross gives them the DNA of their Father. They enter a new family, a new community. Whatever dysfunctional family setting they're in, you show them that they can be positioned into something better—an intimate relationship with God. That's the will of the Father!

Lord, is there anything You wouldn't do for me? Knowing that You were thinking of me on the cross leaves me without words. If You would go to such great lengths, how could I ever doubt Your love, Your care, Your protection. Thank You for saving and restoring me back to You. I am taking hold of the joy of relationship!

Your relational position is your choice, and you get to choose how deep your relationship can be. There is no other place where you can be so open and honest; no other relationship that offers true intimacy and safety. You may think that you have a good relationship with God already. Could it be better? Is there anything that you have on your heart but have been reluctant to bring to Him? Ask Him to show you a fresh aspect of intimacy today.

For further study:
Rom. 5:8; Col. 1:27; I Pet. 1:18-19, 3:18

As you go about your day today, ask the Lord to show you how much He loves you.

DAY 12

God Made It Personal

Behold what manner of love the Father has bestowed on us, that we should be called the children of God!

I John 3:1a

There are so many things I have yet to share about the goal of the cross, but I want to continue to dive into the aspect of relationship, specifically in regard to our witness. As believers, we are called to be living demonstrations of the one true God living inside of us.

In our daily routines, we encounter people who are closed off to "religion." Some may have grown up in church but faded into the world's way of living, or even dabbled in other beliefs or practices. Other times we meet those who've never been introduced to the Gospel or have seen or heard things that weren't too inviting.

This is why I stress the importance of a p intimate, and ever-growing relationship with G in our relationship with Him where we get to know Him and how to effectively live out what H given us. There is a higher dynamic of relation that we can experience because God is not far o left field. God made relationship personal. As we t hold of our relationship with Him, the love and life receive will bubble over onto others.

In I Peter 1:18-19, Peter addresses the Jewish people. *... knowing that you were not redeemed with corruptible things, like silver or gold, from your aimless conduct received by tradition from your fathers, but with the precious blood of Christ, as of a lamb without blemish and without spot.* Peter was speaking to people who were generationally indoctrinated in tradition. Now, the Law itself served its purpose, but Peter was introducing them to a new way they could relate to God—a new wine in a new wineskin. This revelation of the Gospel packaged in

> This revelation of the Gospel packaged in Christ was the new that fulfilled the old. It eliminated the barrier and the level of work required to uphold the Law.

hrist was the *new* that fulfilled the *old.* It eliminated ie barrier and the level of work required to uphold he Law. Jesus became their High Priest. God was not ust the distant God of Abraham, Isaac, and Jacob. God could now truly be called *Father* in every sense of the word!

We see a lot of religions today that are based off rules and regulations, idols and dead gods. But the message of the cross has survived. That's why we make time to cultivate relationship and dive into God's Word. As we grow in the freedom that the Gospel has provided, we share our experiences and our testimonies which can potentially bring freedom to others.

In I John 3:1 we read: *Behold what manner of love the Father has bestowed on us, that we should be called children of God.* Behold! Consider what it cost the Father to restore relationship with us, the price that was paid for us to become His children. No other god has ever sacrificed a son or ever will. God placed such value on His creation that He made a clear pathway to have our sins forgiven and removed. We just say *yes* and believe. The cross has allowed us direct access to Him. This is why we run boldly to the throne room of grace to receive help.

First Corinthians 1:9 says, *God is faithful, by whom you were called into the fellowship of His Son, Jesus Christ our Lord.* When you think of the word fellowship, it is not representative of a fearful subject coming to his master, hoping that he's done enough to win his master's favor. No, fellowship involves intimacy where we can sit and commune with *our* Master. It's a heart-to-heart connection because we are one with Him. We were what He was dreaming up when the redemptive plan was set in motion: *I want to have relationship with them.*

There are people in religions who don't know that God is love and don't realize that Christianity is about a real relationship. When wc share the truth of His nature, these people are astounded. They don't know that He desires to speak to them and guide them. God wants people to know His heart. He is always making movement toward them. He says, "*Call to me and I will answer.*" If we don't fully apprehend the truth of what the cross accomplished, we're going to miss opportunities to share it with the people God has entrusted us with.

First John 4:16 reads: *And we have known and believed the love that God had for us. God is love, and he who abides in love abides in God, and God in him.*

Again, the whole dynamic of the cross is about the revealed love of God. This is why we don't have to be afraid to approach God. We freely give Him access to every part of our hearts and dreams; our agendas and relationships. We don't just have a Sunday morning or Wednesday night encounter, or a chapter-here-and-a-verse-there kind of day. Abiding is daily interaction.

In First John 5:12 it says, *He who has the Son has life; and he who does not have the Son does not have life.* It is only through Jesus that you are granted eternal life. This is what we communicate to others, but it includes that *heaven-on-earth* reality. In Him is every relational miracle, every hope for the broken or missing things in your life. You can draw near to Him as one that dwells in the secret place of the Most High, under the shadow of His wings.

First John 4:13 says: *By this we know that we abide in Him, and He in us, that He has given us of His Spirit.* This is the essence of our relationship. Abiding is interaction. Interaction is what we do in relationships, right? God is not way up there and we're down here. We have a God that is all about us! Knowing that, we in turn are prompted to be about Him. We want to be in the Word, we want to know His heart, we want to hear His voice.

We don't compartmentalize our relationship. We want all of Him and His perfect will for our lives.

A huge part of His will for us is sharing with others what we have received from Him in our own personal relationship. As we share, they will see the fruit of peace and stability. They will witness courage and a heart that stands for truth. They will see a life fully dependent on His love. This is the resurrection power that flows from us onto others. This is the victory that we are called to share!

Lord, I thank You for giving me direct access to Your heart. I have so much that I haven't shared with others; but I am growing and being encouraged by Your Spirit. Thank You for Your Word and everything contained in it. I see how meticulously You have laid out Your plan. I look forward to learning more of what You have for me.

A personal relationship is a tremendous gift, but it needs to be "opened" each day! How does today's study prompt you to cultivate your relationship with God? Who can you invite today to hear what the Lord has revealed to you, or what fulfilled promise can you share with someone? It may be the encouragement someone needs today.

For further study:
Ps. 91:1-4; I Jn. 5:11-12

As you go about your day today, ask the Lord to show you how much He loves you.

DAY 13

Reflection

In another powerful week of devotionals, we've discussed many revelations of what the cross freed you **from** and freed you to **be**. Take time over the next several days to meditate on these key principles.

If you think your sin is too horrible for God, that is pride. In what ways do you let shame, regret, or condemnation from past or current sin keep you from building your relationship with God? Do you recognize any areas where you need to let go of pride and receive the fullness of God's forgiveness?

Because of Christ's death and resurrection, He is the one standing before God and lives to make intercession for us. His priesthood is without end. Understanding that Christ took your place so that you could stand before God pure, how can you draw closer and become bolder in your relationship with God?

DAY 14

Reflection

God lives on the inside of us, and we are called to walk in that reality. You are a born again, spirit-filled child of God! How does this reality look in your life? In what ways and actions do you feel like God is wanting to show Himself through you more?

The cross was not about Him, it was about us. When Jesus was on the cross you were the joy set before Him. He endured the cross to bring us back into relationship with God. Are you willing to realize that nothing you do or don't do qualifies you for salvation but His love alone? What ways have you made your walk with God about you? Are you willing to let go of your performance today and receive the fullness of His gift?

The revelation of the gospel packaged in Christ was the new covenant that fulfilled the old. It eliminated the barrier and the performance required to uphold the law. In what ways have you let the enemy deceive you to think there are barriers to receiving what Jesus did for you? Will you repent today and believe that God's love and blessings depend on His goodness, not yours?

DAY 15

You Can Know

When the Spirit of truth comes, he will guide you into all the truth, for he will not speak on his own authority, but whatever he hears he will speak, and he will declare to you the things that are to come.

John 16:13 ESV

There is truly a blessing that comes when you understand the position of relationship. Again, relationship is one of the reasons Jesus sacrificed His life for you. Some people may feel like salvation is good enough. They've bookmarked the chapter in God's redemption story that promises heaven but have never tapped into the victory they really possess. They might believe that there is a *phase two* of salvation but believe it's beyond their reach because of what they've experienced, and sadly, by what they've been told by so-called spiritual leaders. Listen, there is no phase two. You have been brought into a position of relationship that belongs to you.

When you know the victory that the cross enables you to have, that becomes the place where you can begin to prophesy things concerning your future.

When the devil comes to interrupt your life, He will try to tell you that you can't really know God. Yes, you can! The verse in John 16 above speaks of this outright. The dynamic of intimacy and fellowship constantly invites you to hear the voice of God. He wants you to get His perspective and vision. You have the ability to see beyond the natural. When you know the victory that the cross enables you to have, that becomes the place where you can begin to prophesy things concerning your future. Truth is the only thing the Holy Spirit hears Jesus speak; and it's the only thing He speaks to you. So, when the devil threatens with sickness and disease, or any attack to your mind and emotions, you'll get truth from the Holy Spirit: *I sent my Son, He is constantly making intercession for you. His grace has redeemed your past. He has set you free. You don't have to live with your head hung low. Your future is more than what you are envisioning. You don't have to settle. I am not a man that I should lie!*

You have a relationship with Almighty God—who is victorious. You don't have to worry about the future or what is to become of your life or your purpose. Your competence is in the truth, so you declare truth! The finished work of the cross births a spirit of prophecy.

Isaiah 65:24 reads: *Before they call, I will answer; and while they are yet speaking, I will hear.* This is so powerful because only God can promise something like that. He knows just *when* we are about to call on Him and provides the answer *before* we finish our sentence! In Isaiah 30:21, it says this: *Your ears shall hear a word behind you, saying, "This is the way, walk in it," whenever you turn to the right hand or whenever you turn to the left hand.* This verse promises that we will hear His will, His direction for our lives. The cross paved our future paths. This is the confidence we have in the cross. We never have to fear that we will wander aimlessly or wonder if our lives will make a difference. When we hear His voice, we will know the direction of our steps.

He positioned us in relationship not only because we were chosen to inherit such a great salvation, but to also understand that we are to be fashioned into a spiritual house. This is where you and I now start to reflect the Kingdom of God as a holy priesthood that offers up spiritual sacrifices (I Peter 2:4-5). Sacrifice in this sense means that everything we do is offered at a level of submission. We represent the Kingdom by how we love. We don't follow the dictates of the world—it's not about ego, selfishness, or pride. Rather, we *sacrifice* our agendas and our wills to the authority of God.

We have been given an everlasting covenant through His blood and we are complete in every good work (Hebrews 13:20-21). The cross fulfilled the *old* and ushered in the *new*. This is an everlasting covenant that will never break. This is why you can have confidence in what He tells you to do. You can be saved and have the fullness of the Godhead living within you, but still be constantly distracted by your own life and desires. He didn't make you complete so you could succeed in your own agenda. Within your place of relationship, you are invited to know His very best for your life. You can be confident that everything you touch and every opportunity that knocks will be handled and carried out in a manner that is worthy of Him.

So many believers feel like they're wandering in circles because they don't know the will of God. But this is exactly what the cross came to show. That's why Jesus said, "*If you've seen me, you've seen the Father.*" We can know His heart—He wants us to know it! The more we interact with Him, the more we will mirror His character and nature. We then trust His promises for our lives and understand exactly what we are destined for. We will become more than conquerors through Him who loved us.

The life that we now live is by the faith of the Son of God who loved us and gave Himself for us (Galatians 2:20). Our position of relationship is a beautiful part of the cross. Now we have direct access to the heart of God. We don't ever have to wonder or be fearful of what the devil schemes up next. We declare our victory and show the devil that the cross is the mountain upon which we stand. We speak the truth (the Word) over our lives and for our future.

Our understanding of what the cross provided is so important because there is an unbelieving world we are going to impact. There are also many believers who've allowed religion to dictate the course of their lives. They've held onto wrong mindsets and think that they need to deserve, earn, and then work to keep their right standing with the Father. That kind of religious thinking totally wipes away the victory of the cross.

Christ has called you to know Him. You have not only been positioned in relationship because of His great love for you, but God sees resurrection power in you. As you stay close to Him and know His good, acceptable and perfect will, you will fulfill the commission to declare the Good News of the finished work of the cross.

Lord, now more than ever I am stirred to remain in You because You will lead and guide me into all truth. I am taking ownership of my relationship and owning all the promises of my inheritance. Anytime my flesh comes against Your perfect will, I ask You, Holy Spirit, to remind me to come back to the cross, back into the safety of relationship.

We can fully know the perfect will of God for our lives. We are perfectly positioned where we can receive the fullness of what the cross provided—there is no phase two to our salvation. We just have to believe and receive. Based on the truth of His Word, what things can you start prophesying for your future? For your family? For your calling?

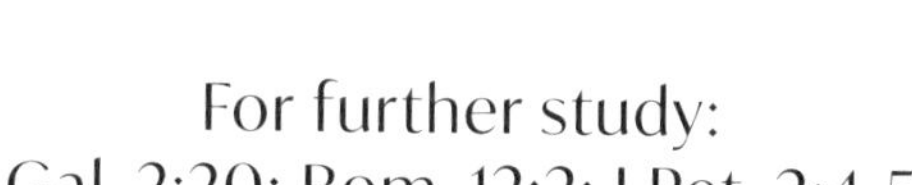

For further study:
Gal. 2:20; Rom. 12:2; I Pet. 2:4-5

As you go about your day today, ask the Lord to show you how much He loves you.

DAY 16

Positioned in the Kingdom

In Him we have obtained an inheritance, have been predestined according to the purpose of him who works all things according to the counsel of his will.

Ephesians 1:11 ESV

Because of the work of the cross, you and I don't have to walk as we once did. We are no longer held captive by the dictates of the flesh and its passions. We now can enjoy a lifestyle rich in the understanding that we have obtained an incredible inheritance. That means full access to all that Christ died for us to have. God *is* the Kingdom. He is positioned in us, and us in Him. Simply stated, this is being positioned in the Kingdom.

This is the Kingdom of His dear Son (Colossians 1:13), this is the Kingdom of the fullness of God. We don't need to wait until heaven; the fullness is for here and now. We were predestined according to the purpose and counsel of His will—created with His power, His creative energy. This is the same will and power that forgave the sins of the entire world. God had us on His heart when He established this redemptive plan. There's a whole world that needs to be reached; and being positioned in the Kingdom is where you and I get to participate in His process.

> We cannot live with a reflection of God's nature if we are not living a surrendered life.

In Ephesians 1:7 it reads: *In Him we have redemption through His blood, the forgiveness of sins, according to the riches of His grace.* Redemption through His blood is what we've been talking about this whole time in regard to the cross. His blood didn't just satisfy the wages of sin but redeemed everything that had been lost because of sin. The New Covenant reality we live in is because of the riches of His grace, and where we forever enjoy true righteousness before the Father.

Continuing on in that same chapter, it reads: *which He made to abound toward us in all wisdom and prudence* (v. 8). The completed work of the cross ushered in our inheritance. It didn't just trickle toward us, but it poured out in all wisdom and foresight. It is an all-encompassing, all-abounding Gospel!

In verse nine it reads: *having made known to us the mystery of His will, according to His good pleasure which He purposed in Himself.* The mystery spoken here consists of prophecies in the Old Covenant that pointed to a coming Messiah. It wasn't just a prophecy that foretold of a virgin birth or that a Messiah would come to rule and reign as a *physical* king. No, this mystery was going to be the full and complete sacrifice that would fulfill the Law and bring in a better covenant with better promises.

He willed Himself to lay down His life so *that in the dispensation of the fullness of the times He might gather in one all things in Christ, both which in heaven and earth—in Him* (v. 10). God had this wonderful plan for man's salvation, but everything would be gathered in His perfect timing. His eternal Kingdom is both in heaven and earth. If people are willing to believe by faith, they will obtain this all-abounding inheritance (v. 11). It doesn't say that one day *in Him* you will obtain. No, it says *now* we have obtained something that was predestined for us to have!

James 2:5 (ESV) says: *Listen, my beloved brothers, has not God chosen those who are poor in the world to be rich in faith and heirs of the kingdom, which he promised to those who love him?* We have been made rich in the faith and heirs of the Kingdom now; it is not for the future. We are not going to need to be rich in faith in heaven. Faith is needed now so that we're able to see past the natural realm. As a rightful heir, we need to take the things of heaven and make them known to the people around us.

Our lives will give evidence to the supernatural. We cannot live with a reflection of God's nature if we are not living a surrendered life. John Maxwell is quoted as saying, *"Live a life that demands a supernatural explanation."* Living from our position of relationship, from our position in the Kingdom, and with the understanding of the goal of the cross, we're empowered to walk in Kingdom realities that manifest the supernatural. The love we minister can set people free (John 8:32). We reveal the glory of God in real, everyday situations. Our confident position as a child will show our victory, our freedom, our authority. Nations will come to our light, and kings will come to the brightness of our dawn (Isaiah 60:3)!

The inheritance we have now was spoken of in Ephesians 2:7 (ESV): *that in the coming ages he might show the immeasurable riches of his grace in kindness toward us in Christ Jesus.* This was written a long time ago, so we are now living *in the ages to come.* This inheritance is for today!

For by grace you have been saved through faith, and that not of yourselves; it is the gift of God, not of works, lest anyone should boast (Ephesians 2:8-9). Do we find ourselves boasting in our works or boasting in the Kingdom of God? Our position empowers us to step out in faith and make bold declarations. We can lay our hands on the sick, and they shall be healed; we shall cast out demons and they will flee. Why? Because we're not doing it with our own power. We have all the working power of the Kingdom of God within us! That's our position. Thanks be to God!

Thank You, Lord, that my position as Your child gives me free access to all that You have provided! Death was once an absolute condition of my former self, which led to hell; but now I have been made alive! I've been brought into covenant relationship and have Kingdom rights, Kingdom potential, and the full authority of God living inside of me. Help me to boldly step out and declare my victory. I want to use the gifts and talents You have given me to reach those You place in my path.

There are people that think everything will be made well *only* when they get to heaven: there won't be sickness and sorrow; there won't be loneliness, hurt, or offense. Those realities are for now! You have the awesome opportunity to participate in God's prophetic process. Will you say *yes* and join forces with me and share the Gospel? The world truly wants to see the Kingdom of God and they want to see it in you! What stirs your heart when you think of all that Kingdom potential inside of you? What are you willing to share today?

For further study:

· Eph. 2:1-2; Col. 1:13

As you go about your day today, ask the Lord to show you how much He loves you.

DAY 17

Lifestyle of Inheritance

I do not cease to give thanks for you, remembering you in my prayers, that the God of our Lord Jesus Christ, the Father of glory, may give you the Spirit of wisdom and of revelation in the knowledge of him.

Ephesians 1:16-17 ESV

Yesterday, I had alluded to a "heaven mentality." Some people carry the mindset that their afflictions, illnesses, relational problems, and spiritual questions will one day be resolved and answered in the *sweet by and by*. This perspective certainly carries hope, and people are actually proclaiming their future with this kind of thinking, which is great! However, there is wisdom, understanding, and a wealth of revelation to be known now. The Apostle Paul addresses this in the Book of Ephesians.

I want to keep talking about what it means to be positioned in the Kingdom. You are not just a random

> His power that resides within us frees us from a religious mentality and keeps us in a thriving and ever-growing relationship.

believer. Some days you may compare yourself with other believers and see yourself as ordinary. That is so far from the truth! You are *extraordinary* because the Kingdom of God lives inside of you. You hold this position because of the finished work of the cross, because of the resurrection of Jesus. You have the utmost value.

Think back to the Old Covenant. The Spirit of God would come *upon* the prophets; He would come *upon* men and women of God. They didn't have a constant indwelling of the Spirit available to them like New Covenant believers do. We can draw a whole other level of power and strength from the Spirit; we can glean wisdom and gain revelation. This is why you and I are extraordinary—we are positioned to know what we possess.

This is why Paul prayed for eyes to be opened and enlightened, *that you may know what is the hope of His calling, what are the riches of the glory of His inheritance in the saints* (v. 18). People generally leave an inheritance for others when they die. That is exactly what Jesus did when He died, He left us an inheritance. Paul adds the word *glory.* This identifies that the inheritance is hefty—there is a magnitude, a weighty substance to it. There is this *exceeding greatness of His power toward us who believe* (v. 19). When you get a revelation of what you possess, you feel confident that God entrusts you to steward that inheritance well. We are to live with a lifestyle of Kingdom revelation, a lifestyle of inheritance.

This is a lifestyle that believes that the cross gave you everything—a lifestyle that responds to God's daily invitation to relationship. There is where we get the opportunity to grow in the knowledge of God. This is the beauty of our relationship. If we don't understand inheritance, or choose not to make the effort to know, we forfeit the truth. We also close the door to the exceeding greatness of His power. He is not holding back. He keeps the flow coming to us, but *only to those who choose to believe.*

When God raised Jesus from the dead and seated Him at His right hand, this demonstrated His mighty power (v. 20). This is the completed work. Remember, when a king sits, his work is done. Jesus is the King of kings and Lord of lords. When He sat, this ushered in our ability to fully know the glory of our inheritance. We can have the Spirit of wisdom and revelation because all of this was given to us in Christ.

The resurrection revealed God's power. When we talk about the death and burial of Jesus, we have to also speak of the resurrection. The goal of the cross wasn't just for Jesus to die, reveal God's love, to fulfill the Law. It just didn't provide us relationship and bring the Kingdom of God into our sights. The resurrection made it possible for the fullness of the Spirit of God to live within us. Now He can release His power and inheritance within us and through us. We don't have to figure out our purposes or do life on our own.

He has promised that He will be with us and abide in us forever. He came to make His home with us. We must always come back to the truth of the cross and what it provided for us. His power that resides within us frees us from a religious mentality and keeps us in a thriving and ever-growing relationship.

My heart breaks when I see people caught up in religion. They haven't got a hold of the truth of the sovereignty of God. Yes, He is mighty and magnificent—an all-consuming fire. All power is within Him, He has no equal. However, His sovereignty is founded by how He makes Himself known. He will not do anything outside of what He has declared in His Word, or anything outside of His character or nature. The purpose of this study is to discover His heart, going line by line, to get to know this great love. His sovereignty revolves around relationship with man and is not fear-based or works-based. It is about what He says is ours and what is within the authority we have been given!

Today, there is wisdom, revelation, and an understanding available to you. You are called to take ownership of and demonstrate a lifestyle of inheritance. What you release to others will offer hope that others become attracted to. You can be the salt and light that reveals who He is, and what He's done.

Lord, I pray that I will remain an open door to all that You have for me. I do want a richer understanding of what my salvation ushered in. By faith, I am choosing to enter the fullness of Your grace, the fullness of Your power, and the fullness of my inheritance.

I trust that this study is helping you come to a place of increasing knowledge and faith in God's Word. His exceeding power that resides in you trumps any lie of the devil. One area that many of us fail to recognize is the power of our words. Can you identify patterns of unbelief that come out of your mouth that defy the truth you have learned today?

For further study:
Matt. 5:13-14; Eph. 1:16-20

As you go about your day today, ask the Lord to show you how much He loves you.

DAY 18

Positioned in the Body of Christ

And may you have the power to understand, as all God's people should, how wide, how long, how high, and how deep his love is.

Ephesians 3:18 NLT

The cross is not only a symbol of our faith, but of victory. If we start to drift from truth, we have the Holy Spirit who hears directly from God to remind us exactly what Jesus did: *Your sin was dealt with;* check. *You're righteous and reconciled;* check. *The Law was fulfilled, no need to strive;* check. *I'm positioned in you and you are in Me;* check. You get the idea.

If you think about it, these truly are accomplishments of the cross. It's important that we discuss these because we need to be able to declare our competence in His victory. What He did for us and what He has provided for us gives us the right to applaud and laud

> We can be confident that we are loved by God, but sometimes He extends His love to you through someone else.

it to the world: *This is my victory!* We give voice to what has been accomplished because the devil, religion, and the world will keep trying to *add to* Jesus' finished work. When we give them our ear, our focus is not on the victory but on ourselves.

As believers, we should want to maintain an attitude of victory, and the best way we can do that is through our position in the Body of Christ, or the church. This is another accomplishment of the cross, but sometimes people carry the attitude: *I love you Jesus; I just don't like Your church.* There may be several reasons why people say this, but for the majority, it is because Christians are *just so much work.* All of us are in different parts of revelation, transformation, and application. We all bring different levels to the Body of Christ; and at times, that can either be a blessing or a strain.

It is important to remember that people are precious to the Lord. You were not the only *joy that was set before Him,* but all those around you were too. God is so delighted when He sees His family link arms with one another because the greater diversity of giftings, perspectives, paths, and testimonies, the greater God's grandeur!

When we as believers bring an array of differences, we bring a tremendous passion and dynamic to ministry. As we interact, we sharpen one another and shore up each other with encouragement and strength. We bring a fuller picture and a fuller experience to the table and eventually see more of the fullness of God together.

The enemy hates the church. When he sees the church uniting, he'll bring discord and frustration. Sometimes, the most intense offense comes from someone you think should know better: *I thought you were a Christian.*

In Ephesians 3:14-20, the Apostle Paul talks about knowing width, the depth, the height and the breadth of God's love; that the people would comprehend with the saints, to become rooted and established together. There is this dynamic of the supernatural that happens when Christians receive a revelation of God's love. We can be confident that we are loved by God, but sometimes He extends His love to you through someone else. Recently, I was given a surprise gift from my personal trainer. She came to me and said, *"God told me to give this gift to you."* The gift was workout gear I wanted to get for myself. She had heard from the Lord, and I got to experience His love through my trainer. I was so blessed!

When we're gathered with other maturing believers, there truly is a momentum to our growth. We start to edify each other because we can identify with someone else's journey. There are many scriptures that talk about friendships in general; but there is something about relationships with others who are heaven-bound. When we share the knowledge of the inheritance, there is an anointing that propels us to draw or pull from each other. This type of friendship is a huge accomplishment of the cross. Jesus died so that we could have healthy and powerful relationships.

In I John 1:3, we read: *that which we have seen and heard we declare to you, that you also may have fellowship with us; and truly our fellowship is with the Father and with His Son….* John was sharing what he had seen and heard as a disciple of Jesus. This account demonstrated fellowship with the readers and invited them to vicariously experience the manifested life of the triune God. John revealed the truth of eternal life even though they didn't have John's firsthand experience. This is the way we came to salvation, right? We had a *secondhand* experience sso to speak, but it was fellowship with the Father, Son, and Holy Spirit nonetheless.

This is why the enemy tries so hard to divide the church. He doesn't like it when we join forces, regardless of if it's in the physical sense or via another means. He especially tries to divide religion. Religion has had such a damaging effect. When we're constantly evaluating and berating ourselves based on performance or insecurity, that same critical spirit can be projected on someone else: *You need to stop that if you want God to heal you. If I'm trying so hard to work toward God, well, you've got a whole list to work on yourself.* This lack of unity and religious criticism is what the enemy is going after. If he can keep believers from being united, then how will we reach the world? The world will know that we are His by the way we love each other (John 13:35).

Ephesians 2:19 reads: … *you are no longer strangers and foreigners, but fellow citizens with the saints and members of the household of God.* I am blessed that I don't have to do my walk with the Lord alone. If I had to, yes, He is enough; but I have the added joy to link arms with like-minded people. That doesn't mean I stay in a Christian bubble. No, I will go out and shine my light to reach the lost and to love extravagantly. People may persecute me and call me crazy, but I will have a whole tribe of crazies with me, growing, learning, and advancing the Kingdom of God together.

We don't want to underestimate our position in the body. We are blessed to be in a community of fellowship that has *been built on the foundation of the apostles and the prophets, Jesus Christ Himself being the chief cornerstone, in whom the whole building, being fitted together, grows into a holy temple in the Lord…* (Ephesians 2:20-21). We are not being built alone but together. When we are willing to be uniquely fitted and joined, there is synergy, energy, life, and power. There is an anointing of His presence, and the gates of hell will not prevail!

Lord, I thank You that my victory lies in You. Help me to appreciate community and see that victory can be greatly multiplied in numbers. Let today be a starting point where I will choose to be fitted and perfected for every good work within the Body of Christ.

Never underestimate what you bring to the table when you unite with others. You have the living God inside of you, so you can draw directly from the One who has everything you need. What is that one thing you could use today in relationships? What about your work environment? Home?

For further study:
I Jn. 1:2-3

As you go about your day today, ask the Lord to show you how much He loves you.

DAY 19

Multiplied Anointing

Again I say to you, if two of you agree on earth about anything they ask, it will be done for them by my Father in heaven.

Matthew 18:19 ESV

As a believer, you have the full backing of heaven in your life. You are a powerful force with the fullness of the Kingdom inside of you; and when you join with other believers, the anointing multiplies. There is creativity and passion that God can use to direct and guide a vision to fruition. The church is called to make incredible Kingdom impact together!

With our position within the Body of Christ, the church can serve with limitless power. I have met many believers as a minister and missionary around the world and it seems that the power of the Gospel has gone missing. These people still serve but they can get easily distracted and do not put a value on the power they have within them. Or others don't have a solid understanding of how powerfully they can be as the Body of Christ.

With revelation comes great peace.

In St. Petersburg, Russia, there was a time when my team and I visited several churches and different ministries. We wanted them to be aware that Charis Bible College was coming to St. Petersburg. As we made our introductions to the leaders of these churches, I asked if they knew the pastors or members of neighboring churches. Many times, the answer was *no.* I thought it interesting that so many didn't know each other. It made me think of a dismembered body: an arm over here, some toes over there; a head beyond the outskirts of the city. Can you imagine the impact those members of the Body of Christ could've made if they were all unified and growing together?

I had shared in another series how my family and ministry family united when my sister was diagnosed with Covid. My peace was a little shaken because the doctors' reports were not promising. But we were all united declaring truth over her—for her health and for her husband and children. I got a hold of Colossians 1:19-20. These were verses that I knew well but revisiting them helped to restore my peace: *For in him all the fullness of God was pleased to dwell, and through him to reconcile to himself all things, whether on earth or in heaven, making peace by the blood of his cross* (ESV). I was reminded of the blood of the cross and reminded of Him who lives in me. My family and I encouraged each other not only with these verses, but many others. This is why it is important to let the beauty of the Gospel resound within our hearts. We grow in the wisdom, knowledge, and the authority we have in Him. We can share the Word to edify and strengthen the body. With revelation comes great peace.

Peace is a powerful force when it comes to our position in the body. I had mentioned in a previous lesson that sometimes Christians are the ones who can offend us the most. Despite how you might have been hurt, peace is part of your victory. I've worked long enough with people to understand that they act *just like people;* they don't act like believers. They still get frustrated and tangled up in their emotions. However, we need to understand that the cross brought us into something so much bigger—it was the Kingdom that He wanted to bring to earth. Not only in us individually, but as the Body of Christ, the church.

I was at a church the other day and I saw a sign placed in the foyer that you were to read as you exited the church: *The church has now left the building.* I loved that because so many times we think of the church as a building or some other structure. The church is the people, heaven displayed on earth. The church is meant to be the community that takes care of widows and orphans; a unified body that brings restoration to the bruised and broken. God is wanting to release His church to demonstrate His will, His desires, His heartbeat to a whole city, to a whole nation. Our opening verse is significant when we talk about multiplied anointing. The verse is about agreement. But if you'll go on to read verse 20, Jesus is speaking: *"For where two or three are gathered together in My name, I am there in the midst of them."* There is power in agreement, there is power in your words. When we are in agreement, He will hear us!

When I left for Russia as a missionary, the team that I was with was amazing. We grew together, served and networked together. It was commonplace for us to push and encourage each other. With our many different strengths and gifts, we all found our places within the team. Because we functioned as a church body should, and had God's direction, we planted a church. There was an ebb and flow of different team members, and we all worked on different teams, at different times, and in different cities. A lot of agreement was involved in this joint venture as well as much prayer. It showed me what the Body of Christ can do when there is unity.

When you are working and trying to do everything for God by yourself, the chances that you'll burn out are likely. What happens when you're discouraged and lonely, or when you get attacks from the enemy? You'll want a fellow believer to edify, strengthen, and encourage you. Yes, you have the Holy Spirit; but God's love is many times extended through human interaction. Working with my team transformed me because of my exposure to others with different levels of maturity and giftings. We were all able to pull on each other's strengths and wisdom. Did I have everything to offer my team? No. But community, participation, and agreement taught me lifelong lessons of what being part of the family of God produces. I got to see a multiplied anointing which blessed me beyond measure!

Lord, thank You for all the people You have placed in my life. When I join my faith with theirs, it grows and multiplies! I want to be found making a Kingdom difference. I pray for wisdom and clarity. Lead me and help me follow the plan You've set for me. Stir within me passion for Your people and Your purposes.

Romans 12:6-8 talks about different gifts of the body. I know people tend to say they don't know their gifts. Many times, you discover your gifts in the *doing*. If you know exactly your specific place and the gifts you bring to the Body of Christ, what are some ways you can help another person discover their gifts?

For further study:
Rom. 1:16; Col. 1:19-20

As you go about your day today, ask the Lord to show you how much He loves you.

DAY 20

Reflection

What a powerful week of discovering the finished work of the Cross in your life. What you've been called into is absolutely astounding! Relationship with God, Kingdom placement and fulfillment, an inheritance, and the family of God. Oh, that we would see daily the riches we already have been given access to! In these next several days, take time to deepen these revelations of the victory and position you've been placed in because of Jesus!

When you know the victory that the cross enables you to have, that becomes the place where you can stand and prophecy things concerning your future. As you look at verses from this past week, what can you prophecy over your life right now? Write those declarations down.

We cannot live as a reflection of God's nature if we are not living a surrendered life. In what areas are you doing your own thing, not surrendering to God's will and promises for your life? What areas do people see your nature instead of God's nature? Would you be willing to release these areas to God to be transformed?

DAY 21

Reflection

We can be confident that we are loved by God but sometimes He sends His love to you through someone else. In what ways has God used someone recently to reveal His love to you? What are some ways you can show God's love to someone today? Who does He want to show Himself to today through you?

With revelation from the Word of God comes great peace. What revelations in this study have brought a sense of peace and excitement? Take time to record some of the things the Holy Spirit is stirring in your heart!

DAY 22

Positioned in the World for the World

For in Him dwells all the fullness of the Godhead bodily; and you are complete in Him, who is the head of all principality and power.

Colossians 2:9-10

You are positioned in the world for the world. We are privileged to connect with the Body of Christ and take back territory. Territory refers to lost souls. We make a stand and tell the devil that he can't have them—that territory is off-limits. Be encouraged that you are here for such a time as this.

Now, free will is yours to exercise and you may think: I'm a child of God, I'm going to heaven. I really don't have any gift or talent. Others are more qualified to do the work of the Kingdom. God purposely planted you here for this time in history. How you see yourself and your position in the body is not to be taken casually. If you truly believe you don't have anything to contribute, that is not only an immature perspective, but a lie. In you dwells the fullness of the Godhead bodily; and you are complete in Him. You're empowered because you have the Spirit of God inside of you.

Again, you're positioned in the world for the world. Let me be clear, you are in the world, but you are no longer led by the world's mentalities, desires, passions, or excuses. You're no longer submitting to the prince of the air (Ephesians 2:2). We are new creations in Christ, old things are passed away; all things have become new (II Corinthians 5:17). We still have a physical body, physical attributes, and natural tendencies. However, we are made whole in Him. So that means who you are today and who you are becoming is imperative. There are too many people abdicating God's call on their life.

> The cross and resurrection have equipped us with an identity, an authority, and an ability to influence this world.

I am passionate about people surrendering to a relationship with God. It is actually in relationship where we continue to grow and discover our gifts and our callings for every season of our lives. If we don't value and cultivate relationship with Him, we undoubtedly will blend in with the world.

The cross and resurrection have equipped us with an identity, an authority, and an ability to influence this world. My daughter saw this t-shirt the other day that read: *Make Heaven Crowded!* Of course, I got it for her. Making heaven crowded has got to be our motivation. Our lives are like a vapor in the light of eternity (James 4:14). The short time we are given to be on earth should compel us to take as many souls as possible to heaven with us. Regardless of our occupations, status, gender, or age, we can influence those around us.

In Mark 16:15, we find Jesus commissioning His disciples to go into all the world and preach the Gospel to every creature. As believers, we are called to the same; however, if we don't know the power of the cross, we don't have a message.

I knew that I was called to be a missionary when I was young; and when I thought I was ready, I would ask God when He would release me to go. I remember I had asked *When?* on several occasions. God eventually told me, "*You don't have a message.*" I was a believer, I read the Bible constantly, and I truly loved the Lord.

God showed me that I didn't know how to articulate my passion. I didn't know how to communicate it. He couldn't send me until I was equipped.

When you can see the beauty of the cross, you see the power of it (Romans 1:16). You see God's heartbeat through it. What He accomplished, what was fulfilled, and what He put inside of you is continually bathed with thanksgiving, reinforced with scripture, confirmed with testimonies, and fortified by your relationship with others in the body. You become fully persuaded that God is the God He says He is and you know there is a dying world that needs to know what you know. If you don't fully understand foundational principles, you don't have a message.

Unfortunately, a lot of people teach from a religious platform because they don't know the message of the Gospel; they don't know what the cross truly accomplished. So, they perpetuate and teach what they have been taught, what they know: *You have to do this. You can't do that. You have to pray this way.* We are not commissioned to go out and preach religion.

Mark 16:17 says that signs will follow those who believe. It is all about **believing** what Jesus did, not what we believe we can do on our own. Recall Ephesians 1:19

that says there is this exceeding greatness toward us who believe. So, we go believing that we are empowered with authority to lay our hands on the sick, to speak with new tongues, to cast out demons. We believe that we can draw on the Holy Spirit and become a conduit for His power. What God does through us becomes a demonstration of His love for others *through* us.

When we go as representatives of His glory—with signs and wonders following—the world will stop and say, "*What was that?*" That is when we get to testify of a loving God that sacrificed His Son and encourage them to have their own intimate relationship with Him.

Supernatural signs are like a dinner bell to those who are hungry. You can tell that people crave the supernatural, just look at the movie posters that advertise magic, horror, and the demonic. People will spend their time and money witnessing something beyond their imagination. Moviemakers spend millions to create one superhero movie and invest in the latest and greatest technology to create the illusion of power and might.

You are in this world for such a time as this. You've got a *superhero*—the Almighty God—living inside of you. You have gifts, you have His promises, and you have His Word. You have the whole armor of God ensemble (Ephesians 6:13-17); how cool are you? We are positioned for this time, positioned for the people in our spheres of influence. When we believe in the Gospel and all that has been accomplished, we have a message. We have territory to take back in the name of Jesus!

Lord, help me develop a hearing ear so that I can hear when You direct me to people, places, and into situations where Your love needs to be demonstrated. I don't want to feel inferior but empowered. Even though someone may not respond to what I share with them, You will see that the seeds I sow will be watered. Thank You that You have entrusted me with the Gospel!

When we invited Jesus to be Lord, we essentially said, *"Lord, I surrender my life to You and now my life no longer is mine but Yours."* Do you see yourself, your giftings, your purpose for such a time as this? How *hungry* are you to influence and bring others to God's saving grace? If your *appetite* is not where you know it could be, how can you make room for the Holy Spirit to encourage your heart today?

For further study:
Mk. 16:17-18; Eph. 1:19, 2:2, 6:10-19

As you go about your day today, ask the Lord to show you how much He loves you.

DAY 23

Equipped for Every Season

His divine power has granted to us all things that pertain to life and godliness, through the knowledge of him who called us to his own glory and excellence.

II Peter 1:3 ESV

I pray that every believer would hunger for the purpose of God on their life—to have a passion that wakes them up every morning to say, *"Not my life but Yours, Lord. Here I am, use me today."*

This chapter in your life may be a busy one, but even in the midst of it, don't make an excuse. Life may seem to have brought you to a stalemate where you feel like you're just treading water, but you still can be at the right place, at the right time. When you invite the power of God into a particular season—even the mundane and uneventful—what God can do *through* you is supernatural. He's a creative God; is anything too mundane for Him?

Revelations are the innermost details straight from the heart of God, unique to our individual lives, and are for the purposes of walking in His will in this world.

You may find that this season might be a perfect time to go back to the foundations of your faith. I had previously stressed that if you don't have a full understanding of what the finished work of the cross has provided, you don't have a message to share. Our opening verse leaves us without excuse. He has granted us all things that pertain to life and godliness. There are basic things we keep going back to in the Word, and we keep building upon them. When we fully understand them, they become revelations. Revelations are the innermost details straight from the heart of God, unique to our individual lives, and are for the purpose of walking in His will in this world.

We may encounter believers who crave to see the miraculous. They crave supernatural signs and wonders. They crave but don't have a foundational understanding of who Jesus is. They don't value a personal relationship with Him; therefore, they are not committed to Him.

It is easy to become a flakey Christian, following every wind of doctrine (James 1:6). They don't know who they are in Christ.

But because of what Jesus has done, we know the Gospel message. We have something substantial to disciple someone with. The great commission is your call (Matthew 28:19-20); but that doesn't mean you interrupt the roles where your attention is needed. The question is, what can you do? What impact can you make right now? How can you use your gifts and calling where you are in this season, in your area of the world?

You are equipped to be used by God in whatever season you find yourself in. Your equipping has been founded on the Word: you've had one-on-one personal training in relationship, you have labored with and have been strengthened by those in the household of God, and you have a Life Coach that is ready to guide and lead you. This world will pass away, but what you do for the Kingdom is eternal. You are equipped to demonstrate the signs and wonders of God.

In I Corinthians 2:12, it reads: *Now we have received, not the spirit of the world, but the Spirit who is from God, that we might know the things that have been freely given to us by God.* The spirit of the world will try to downplay what we already have been given. It will tell you what you are not, what you don't have, what you don't know, and what you cannot become. But we know that Jesus did it all and we can know His truth for our lives. His divine power has given us all things that pertain to life and godliness (II Peter 1:3).

This is what you and I possess. This is why you are in this world for such a time as this. Your hands may be in very important things, but again, when you invite God to be at the center of your season, He will stir your creativity. You have so much that you probably haven't tapped into. Don't let the enemy fool you into thinking you don't have the time or energy. Don't let him tell you that you can only watch the game of life from the sidelines or that you can only be a cheerleader. You are not lacking. You are a New Covenant believer with the resurrected Savior living in your heart. You have the Word of God, His promises, and His nature. Your inheritance is for every season of your life.

Second Peter 1:4 reads: *by which have been given to us exceedingly great and precious promises, that through these may be partakers of the divine nature.* You and I are not supposed to just be watching God try to do something. We're partnering with God; so, the things we do reveal and demonstrate the true nature of God. We're revealing the Father, the healer; we're revealing peace. We partake in the divine nature. That is an absolute honor.

Finishing off verse four, it tells us that we have escaped corruption that is in the world. We are in this world but escaping its lies. We escape the idea that says you can only have *this* if you make this much money; you can only succeed if you have this education. We are told in Colossians 2:8 not to be taken captive by this world's philosophies, their system of thinking. It is all empty deceit. What we do for the Kingdom is not about us, it's not about fulfilling our selfish motives, or doing anything that doesn't line up with the Word.

We have a God who understands us in every season of life. His Word is our manual—our road map that helps us stay on course and gives us escape routes if we need them. Stop looking at social media platforms as your compass. You have been positioned in the season you're in and equipped to fulfill what God is calling you to. You can make an impact because you carry the very presence of God.

Lord, there are times that I have placed a higher priority on other pressing matters. I have allowed things to trip me up and have allowed myself to slip in and out of relationship with You. Understanding that You've equipped me for the season I'm in empowers me; I see things in a different light. Thank You for bringing my focus back where it should be.

We all have things that are so immediate that we can sometimes lose focus. That's never a surprise to God. But as you become increasingly aware that He is for you, what measures can you take that will help you return to your Source? Is there another believer you can be accountable to?

For further study:
Matt. 28:19-20; Eph. 4:14;
Jas. 1:6; II Pet. 1:4

As you go about your day today, ask the Lord to show you how much He loves you.

DAY 24

Anointed for Persecution

But even if you should suffer for righteousness' sake, you will be blessed. Have no fear of them, nor be troubled.

I Peter 3:14 ESV

As believers, our lives should reflect God's love, His character, and nature. There should be something very distinct about us that makes us stand out from the world. It doesn't matter if we know how to defend the Bible or defend the tenets of the faith. If no one can see a marked difference or asks what the reason for our hope is, that's a problem.

I recently taught a leadership lesson at Charis Bible College and was ministering something similar. We should look totally opposite of this world; we should look like Jesus. Many times, we will run into someone or a people group that doesn't like what they see

When we don't let persecution harm our hearts and minds, it loses its power.

or what we represent. Our lives should reflect the cross, the truth of the Gospel, and reflect what the promises declare over our lives. Even when we have not done a thing to them, their offense is stirred by their sinful nature. They carry the attitude of mockery: *I want to do what I want to do.*

We are seeing persecution of Christians all over the world like never before. Now, there has been extreme persecution in the past if we look at history, but we are hearing how people have been slaughtered for their faith in foreign nations. Here at home, we see persecution on the rise, especially the ridicule and disdain for what we believe and how our position goes against worldly principles.

It is so important to have such a love and a revelation of the cross so that when we are called to abandon our stance or compromise our beliefs, we're able to emphatically say *no!* What Jesus did for us is worth more than the approval of this world. When we grasp what the cross provided, it creates a tenacity and an attitude of boldness. An uncompromising spirit rises because we know how we were purchased. We have value in God's eyes. We need to come to a place where we declare, *"I will not lower myself to ungodly standards, mentalities, or regulations. I am worth more than that."*

People will tell us to stop preaching the cross. They either don't believe God exists or believe there is more than one way to God: *You can take your little Christianity message elsewhere; you can't tell me I'm going to hell because I don't believe in your Jesus.* In a simple but loving way, we can point them to John 14:6 where Jesus says that He is the way, the truth, and the life. No one can come to the Father any other way. The message of the cross has to become so powerful in our understanding because that verse in John might become the one message we'll get to minister to that person. We cannot just drop it and tell them, *"Oh well, you go figure it out; do whatever you want!"* No, our hearts should burn for the lost just like God's heart, so we are compelled to speak the truth. No matter the retort or rejection, we are not to fear or be troubled. If we don't give them the opportunity to hear truth, when they die, they will go to hell.

In I Peter 3:15, it reads: *But sanctify the Lord God in your hearts, and always be ready to give a defense to everyone who asks you a reason for the hope that is in you, with meekness, and fear.* This is a powerful verse that I use a lot when I teach Apologetics. Apologetics comes from *apologia* which means to give a defense. Giving a defense is like what I explained about not having a message. If you cannot articulate the message of the cross, you will not be able to articulate your defense well.

I remember traveling to India as a teen with a missionary medical team. After getting there, we had to travel on rough terrain to get to a certain village. The journey was long so it gave the medical crew and me the chance to talk with our host team. It was surprising to hear from the host team that the village we were going to had never heard of the message of Jesus.

When we got to the village, I noticed all the kids were carrying Coca-Cola and Fanta bottles. This was troubling to me: *Coca-Cola and Fanta made it to the village before Jesus did?*

The team and I eventually were able to be the first to introduce Jesus to that village. Praise God! But if I had known then what I know now about the Gospel, I could have given a much simpler and much clearer defense for my faith. My articulation would have been so much better.

Regardless of our defense, people will revile us, pick Christianity apart, and call us evil (v. 16). They will point a finger at us to take the attention off the evil they are doing themselves. We see this happening now in politics, families, businesses. It is rampant, but we mustn't let their evil work touch our hearts; we must stay the course: *I may get reviled for my faith, but I know my God and I have joy in my salvation!*

In I Peter 4:12-13 it reads: *Beloved, do not think it strange concerning the fiery trial which is to try you, as though some strange thing happened to you; but rejoice to the extent that you partake of Christ's sufferings, that when His glory is revealed, you may also be glad with exceeding joy.* In that same leadership class at Charis, I shared with the students that as believers, we don't just throw our hands up every time problems come along, or huff and puff how everyone is against us. Instead, we act like a leader and say, *"Problems are going to come my way, but I'm anointed to handle them. God's not bringing suffering toward me."*

There is a lost and hurting world, but we don't get surprised how their emptiness or shallowness brings attacks to our person. And we don't blame God for them. He is not the one who brings suffering; it is the evil one behind the attack. When people follow the world's way and its ideologies, that is what will dominate their thinking and their belief systems. They eventually journey down into more ungodliness. When we face any trial, we can be certain of God's love and be certain that the devil is at work. We can have an attitude of victory because the devil has no power to disturb our peace.

I'm reminded of my favorite music video as a kid. The Christian artist was named Carman and he played the role of a young Christian man who walked into a male witch's house. The witch was coming against the young man's faith by telling him lies of who God was, and told him that as a Christian, he didn't have any power. He went on to remind the man of his past sins and that he really wasn't saved: *How could God love you?*

There were demons around, rejoicing when the witch spoke. At first, the young man was afraid; but then the music part of the video kicked in. The young man was singing about the blood of Jesus and the victory of the cross. He told the witch that *he* was the one without any power. Every time the man was reminded of his past, he reminded the devil of his future.

As kid, that was powerful, and it depicted what Christians are experiencing now. Knowing that the devil is going to burn forever should give us all the reason to rejoice because we won't be there with him. We don't need to get disheartened when we are ridiculed for our faith or are falsely accused. You can be sure that when we make a stance, there will be some fiery trial; but we've been anointed for persecution. This is an accomplishment of the cross, we don't have to fear what comes against us. When we don't let persecution harm our hearts and minds, it loses its power. We know how the story ends for the devil. People may blaspheme our God; but in our hearts, He is glorified.

Lord, if I am reproached for the name of Christ, I will be blessed for the Spirit of glory and of God rests on me! The world is growing more intolerant of Christians, and I want to be secure in You. Thank You for the Word, Your Son, and the Holy Spirit. When I am confident that You are with me, I don't need to be afraid.

Sometimes we may not want to think about the possibility of suffering the same fate as other faithful Christians, but the reality does exist. If there is any hint of uneasiness or fear, I recommend that you fall in love with the Word all over again and keep the cross consistently in your remembrance. You have the living

God inside of you. There is no fear in Him. What other attributes of God can you list and meditate upon that will help settle any fear?

For further study:
Jn. 3:16; I Pet. 4:14

As you go about your day today, ask the Lord to show you how much He loves you.

DAY 25

Positioned over the Enemy

For whatever is born of God overcomes the world. And this is the victory that has overcome the world—our faith. Who is he who overcomes the world, but he who believes that Jesus is the Son of God?

I John 5:4-5

When Jesus was on the cross, *we* were the joy that was set before Him (Hebrews 12:2). However, I believe He also found joy in something else. Not only did He know that He was defeating the enemy, not only was He going to take the keys of sin, hell, and death—I believe He had the joy of being able to see His people walk in healing, prosperity, and life! Jesus redeemed the authority that Adam gave up and gave it to back to us.

There are people that think the enemy is a mighty, evil beast that can overpower them. He will attempt to give you that idea. He tries presenting himself as a regal, demonic force, but he is a defeated foe, and he knows it—demons even tremble. When we stand at the end of this earthly existence, we'll get a glimpse of the enemy in the deepest part of the pit and consider, *"Can this be the one who terrorized the earth and its kingdoms? Is this the destroyer of its cities; who shut up his prisoners to a living death?"* Because of our position over the enemy, we don't have to wait and see. We can know because God declared his fate in His Word.

Maybe you understand the concept of your position, but you feel that your whole life is nothing but fear. You fear for your family, you're fearful about your marriage. You're fearful about the government and the future of your nation. Fear is not part of your new DNA as a child of God. When we go back and study foundational truths, we continue to build on the strength of that foundation. When fear, dread, or any attack comes our way, we won't be caught off guard; we will have something solid to fall back on. We are to have a foundation that is built on God's Word.

Truth cannot just remain on the pages of our Bibles. We need to employ it in our words, our prayers, and in our actions.

I want us to dive into more verses because I believe there is something that we need to actively understand: *we are not just hearers of the Word, we're doers.* Truth cannot just remain on the pages of our Bibles. We need to employ it in our words, our prayers, and in our actions.

In II Timothy 1:7 it says, *For God has not given us a spirit of fear, but of power and of love and a sound mind.* I already stated that fear is not part of you who are as a child of God. Fear has torment (I John 4:18). Fear is everything that is dark; and what communion has light with dark (II Corinthians 6:14)? You have a spirit of love because the person of love lives within you. Love conquers, love motivates, love is your foundation. Love is the demonstrated glory of God. You have a sound mind because you've been given the Holy Spirit as a teacher who's going to lead and guide you into all truth and understanding. A sound mind is based on something that's stable. You're not of this world and its mentalities anymore; however, you have to renew your mind (Romans 12:2). Renewing your mind involves intentionality. You have to tell your mind what it can and cannot dwell on.

People will ask about mental conditions. When we talk about a sound mind, it is first understanding that Christ died to redeem every illness and every evil work. When you as a believer have that revelation, that is when you soak yourself with teachings about *Who* lives inside of you. We have touched on this; it is God who indwells the believer. Again, mind renewal is intentional. When the medical community says you have a mental disease and that *you will always be bipolar*, or that *you will always suffer from anxiety*, those are "labels" that go against what the Word says. Your victory—your sound mind—is in the finished work of the cross. You no longer have to live your life defined by the condition but *condition* your life to live by every word that proceeds from the mouth of God. You are positioned over the enemy, so you don't have to live in depression, worry, or anxiety. You and I are to live with the stability of thought, heart, and emotion.

First John 5:4 says that *whatever is born of God overcomes the world*. That's powerful. We could go into all the verses that talk about our identity—that we are His redeemed and beloved children. We're positioned over the enemy, so we are overcomers—overcomers that are in this world but not of it. We are not held captive by its dictates or vain philosophies.

Verse 4 goes on to say that *the victory that overcomes the world is our faith*. Faith begins the moment of salvation. We had to have faith to receive Jesus as our Savior. Now, our hope is anchored in the Word, in the accomplishments of the cross, and in our identity as a child of God. Faith grows in relationship with the Holy Spirit. He directs our steps as we walk out our faith. When the world throws us bad reports, or tries to shake us with fear or persecution, our victory is our faith: *No matter what is happening around me, I know how God sees me. I know what I've been given. I know who lives within me.*

(v. 5) *Who is he who overcomes the world, but he who believes that Jesus is the Son of God?* We all are overcomers because we believe; we all have been given His authority. Again, I believe this is part of the joy that Jesus was seeing while on the cross: *They're going to overcome and walk in healing, prosperity, and life simply because they've chosen to believe in what I'm doing for them right now.* I can also imagine that at His trying moment in the Garden of Gethsemane, we were the ones behind His declaration: *Not My will but Yours be done!* There was something bigger at stake: lives! He placed value on our lives and the lives of the whole world. We were seen as worthy.

Romans 8:31 reads: *What shall we say to these things? If God is for us who can be against us?* Some of you may feel that everything is against you—everything appears to be coming at you from all sides. Your hope may be waning because you feel worn out. God says, "*Who can be against you?*" I want to encourage you that no matter what is going on in your life, He wants you to remember what was demonstrated on the cross. He took your place; He took your sin, guilt, and shame—past, present, and future. He has solutions for what you are going through now. He is that powerful and that good. One sacrifice easily took care of the enemy. You can walk tall with that revelation. The cross made a way for you to be positioned over the enemy. Only you can bow and release your God-given authority; only you can allow the enemy to deceive you. People perish for lack of knowledge. If you choose to stop growing, if you choose to stop pursuing the things of God, your victory can seem beyond your reach. And if that has been your experience, look up at the cross!

As I have been sharing God's Word and my heart with you on this journey, I believe we have been growing together. There is always more to learn, there is always room to grow. Anytime we choose to sit under the Holy Spirit, all we have to do is ask Him to lead us and show us the power that is at work inside of us. We are to be salt and light and a witness; but we powerfully demonstrate that we are *more* than conquerors in Christ when we hold onto hope during the most gut-wrenching circumstances. This shows the faithfulness of our God and that His Word is trustworthy. Our position over the enemy is because of the cross. And because the Spirit of God is for us, we can look squarely at situations and tell the devil, "*You are a defeated foe! My faith, my hope, and my victory are found in the one true God!*"

My prayer for you today is that you would know the exceeding greatness of His power that is yours (Ephesians 1:19). You get to choose to believe this or not. No one can believe it for you. What shall you say to these things? Say *yes!* No matter what the enemy has tried to steal, kill, and destroy, you have the victory for your life today.

Lord, I am making more room to grow and to learn from You today. Show me the power that is in work inside of me.

Is there a particular verse that touched your heart and invites you to dig deeper? The Bible tells us to be a doer of the Word. How will you actively *do* that particular verse today?

For further study:
Is. 14:16, 53:5; Jn. 3:3, Rom. 12:2;
II Cor. 6:14; Eph. 1:19; I Jn. 4:18

As you go about your day today, ask the Lord to show you how much He loves you.

DAY 26

Positioned with Authority

Most assuredly, I say to you, he who believes in Me, the works that I do he will do also; and greater works than these he will do because I go to my Father.

John 14:12

Each day offers an opportunity to see a fresh aspect of the finished work of the cross—what Jesus' death, burial, resurrection, and ascension provided for you. When you understand those things, you will have confidence, boldness, and an awareness that you do not live your life on your own. You have the Spirit of the living God dwelling inside of you.

Because He is positioned in us, we are called to apprehend this exceeding great power. This power makes it possible to live victoriously in the Kingdom, in the Body of Christ, in the world, and in our position

> The authority you possess gives you the right to reject every physical and spiritual attack. This is a promise and God will keep His Word.

over the enemy. I want to stir in you the importance of continuing to understand all the principles and key scriptures we've unpacked in this study. Today, I want to put an emphasis on authority because, unfortunately, most people don't have a clue how to exercise it.

Authority was given to us through the blood of Jesus. This was a costly gift. Jesus redeemed the authority that Adam surrendered and gave it to us. Now you and I can go into all the world and make disciples; we can walk in the authority to cast out demons, heal the sick and cleanse the lepers. We freely have received; therefore, we freely give. You and I have so much to give today.

But understanding your authority is key. We have been positioned over the enemy to exercise our authority. This was the joy Jesus envisioned for us. We don't need to walk around bullied and defeated. Jesus saw us taking that authority and running with it!

Now, I know there is a lot of crazy stuff going on in the world. There's plenty to get distracted by, and still more that tries to attack you on a daily basis. You may say, *"I love the idea of the cross and I do have Jesus in my heart; but why is it that I struggle with so many difficulties? I feel I'm constantly being attacked."* When we received Christ as our Savior, we immediately became targets of the enemy. Obviously, we were targets before salvation. It doesn't matter whether people are saved or lost; male or female; adult or child; he just wants us dead—physically or dead to our pursuits, purposes, and passions. Whatever he does to accomplish his mission, death is his goal. When we understand his corrupted nature, we don't need to get fearful or discouraged.

In John 10:10, we read how the enemy comes and tries to steal, kill and destroy; but if you read further Jesus says, *"I have come that they may have life, and that they may have it more abundantly."* The cross revealed God's giving heart, His abundant grace. Abundant life is the truth we hold onto; it is part of the inheritance that we freely have access to and freely live in. So, when the enemy tries to steal our peace, kill our vision, or destroy our purpose, we emphatically remind him that God is the author of these things, He's the author of our lives.

First Peter 5:8 reads: *Be sober, be vigilant because your adversary the devil walks about like a roaring lion, seeking whom he may devour.* This verse *isn't* saying how big the devil is; rather, it is showing you how powerful your God is. This passage says the enemy is *like* a roaring lion. You have the lion of the tribe of Judah living inside of you. You have the King of kings and the Lord of lords. When Jesus said, *"It is finished,"* every foe, every demonic force, every evil plan lost its power.

The devil only roars deception, manipulation, disease. The enemy never roars anything good, and it is always goes against the Word of God. You can say *I don't receive that lie. I know what is written, and I know the price Christ paid for the inheritance I own.* This is exercising your authority. Authority is not yelling, *"In the name of Jesus,"* after every promise in the Bible. If you don't understand the truth, you don't have faith to agree with a promise. In other words, your authority has no power or faith attached to it.

Truth has to be the foundation of our faith. This is why we discuss, study, and consider the cross. Faith doesn't develop after a one-time Bible lesson or Sunday sermon. Faith comes by hearing and hearing by the Word of God (Romans 10:17). When you get a hold of truth, you can say, *"Because of what Jesus did, I have authority over the devil and his attacks."*

I have been encouraging my kids to use their authority when any opportunity arises. My son Michael had recently been experiencing some head cold symptoms. The other night, his coughing and hacking woke me at two o'clock in the morning. I went to his room to check on him. He went into more of a hacking fit and complained of aches and pains. I started to sleepily rebuke the symptoms—*yawning* them to leave in Jesus' name. Michael was looking and feeling miserable. That's when this momma bear woke up: *You know what, devil? Enough!*

In that instant, I got firm and spoke against the attack: *"Devil, you get out of this room, I command you to get your hands off his body and lungs. Michael, you are healed and whole and restored. There's no pressure in your ears, no pain in your throat. It is done in Jesus' name. Devil, who do you think you are?"*

I've noticed something when I get serious with the devil—my son's faith responds. I can see it in his eyes, I see it in how he leans in. And at that early morning rebuke session, I saw his attitude change: *Yeah...yeah, devil; who do you think you are?* When my son started to agree and added his own rebuke, guess what? His ears stopped hurting. He stopped coughing and went back to sleep. It wasn't because of my attitude; it was because his attitude got stirred up. That is so awesome!

We can have a revelation of our authority and our position over the enemy, but the devil does not let up. He will seize any moment to mess with us. What we need to consistently do is to stir up our authority. We don't just passively *chat* with the enemy and hope he responds to us: *Will you please just leave me alone?* If we talk like that, we become the devil's playground. We have authority over the devil. That is our victory.

Revelation brings an attitude. Why? Because the devil is infringing on our rights as a child of God—he is trying to infiltrate Kingdom territory. There has to be a constant stirring of our attitudes, and that is something a lot of people don't do. People tend to tolerate things. I am not saying that people don't believe or stand in faith; but with your faith, **add some attitude.** Stir up that authority.

Some things may seem so minor that we let an attack continue. Have you ever done that? Were you ever a week into a cold, or experiencing some pain in your body and then realized that you hadn't even considered praying about it? Or do you see that the cards are just not in your favor on some issue? What is the natural response? You get into fix-it mode. You start to plan and adjust; or you see that the inevitable is just around the bend, so you let things run their natural course. I believe the Lord is telling us to stop fixing our eyes on what is seen and to shift our eyes to the unseen (II Corinthians 4:18).

First Peter 5:9 (ESV) reads: *Resist him, firm in your faith, knowing that the same kinds of suffering are being experienced by your brotherhood throughout the world.* Resisting and standing in faith helps you to keep the devil from making your suffering all about you: *No one knows what I'm going through. They don't understand; they've never been in my shoes.* You need to keep your focus on God and then reach out to those who are suffering like you. You resist the devil together. You remind each other of the victory and the authority that you possess. Prayer begins to happen; ministry gifts are put in place. You didn't go the route of the devil. You submitted your issues to God, resisted the devil, and the devil had to flee (James 5:7).

Isaiah 54:17 reads: *No weapon formed against you shall prosper, and every tongue which rises against you in judgment, you shall condemn. This is the heritage of the servants of the Lord.* Jesus took care of every weapon. The authority you possess gives you the right to reject every physical and spiritual attack. This is a promise and God will keep His Word.

I will finish with John 14:12. *Most assuredly, I say to you, he who believes in Me the works that I do he will do also; and greater works than these will he do because I go to my Father.* This was one of the goals of the cross, this was an accomplished victory. He says, "*Not only am I going to the cross to take all sin and every evil work, but I am going to My Father, sit down at His right hand and say, 'It is finished.' There is no more barrier between us.*"

You are in the world for such a time as this, and greater things you will do. He says *greater* because He lives within you. So many times, people think that there isn't anything great happening in their life. God can be in that uneventful season; you just need to invite Him.

When you know the value that has been placed on you, you will place a high value on what Jesus suffered, died, and rose for you to have. He did what He did for you, it wasn't about Him. I pray that if you have allowed yourself to be overwhelmed by the enemy that this study brought you back to truth—that you will start to see yourself and any situation through the eyes of the eternal.

Lord, Your cross, my victory! That is my banner in Jesus' name!

My desire is to see you walk in the inheritance, the authority, and the victory that is yours today! Truly, the devil has no power over your life, so don't allow him to think he does! His roar is more of a kitten's meow; it's all in how you perceive it. Be encouraged that you are Jesus' joy; there is nothing that you have done or anything you could ever do that will make God change His mind about you. He eternally loves you. Wrap your mind around that and imagine how that exactly looks like. You'll be amazed at what He brings to your mind!

For further study:
Jn. 15:13

As you go about your day today, ask the Lord to show you how much He loves you.

DAY 27

Reflection

We have had another powerful week of studying the accomplishments of the cross in your life. Getting ahold of these truths brings not only revelation, but an attitude. An attitude of knowing the love of God over you, your victory, inheritance, and authority is key to demonstrating the spirit of God in you! The devil is shaking in his boots as you are getting ahold of these truths! You are filled with the abundant life of God. Now be bold, be passionate, unapologetic in your love of the truth and its freedom. Look at these key principles we've meditated on this last week. How can you continue to let them transform your thinking and stir your passion for God?

The cross and resurrection have equipped us with an identity, an authority, and an ability to influence this world. With the salvation you received in Christ, how are you letting the Holy Spirit use you to influence this world?

The revelations you have received are powerful, straight from the heart of God, unique to our individual lives, and are for the purpose of walking in His will in this world. What revelations has the Lord been speaking to your heart? How are you applying those revelations to the situations and opportunities in your life right now?

It is important to have a love and revelation of the Cross so that when we are called to abandon our stance or compromise our beliefs, we are able to emphatically say no! In what ways have you been pressured subtly or aggressively to abandon your stance or voice the truth? In what ways can you begin to respond differently to these pressures?

DAY 28

Reflection

Truth cannot just remain on the pages of our Bibles. We need to employ it in our words, our prayers, and our actions. What are some key promises that you feel God is speaking to you? In what ways are you going to actively incorporate them into your words, prayers, and actions today?

The authority you possess gives you the right to reject every physical and spiritual attack. This is a promise and God will keep His Word. In any situation, attack, or pressure you're facing right now, speak to it that it holds no power or authority over you! Speak the Word and believe the enemy is fleeing. Take a few moments and write out your declarations of victory and rebuke the devil in any area you're facing right now. Be bold!

Receive Jesus as Your Savior

Choosing to receive Jesus Christ as your Lord and Savior is the most important decision you'll ever make!

God's Word promises, *"That if thou shalt confess with thy mouth the Lord Jesus, and shalt believe in thine heart that God hath raised him from the dead, thou shalt be saved. For with the heart man believeth unto righteousness; and with the mouth confession is made unto salvation"* (Romans 10:9–10 KJV). *"For whosoever shall call upon the name of the Lord shall be saved"* (Romans 10:13 KJV). By His grace, God has already done everything to provide salvation. Your part is simply to believe and receive.

Pray out loud: "Jesus, I confess that You are my Lord and Savior. I believe in my heart that God raised You from the dead. By faith in Your Word, I receive salvation now. Thank You for saving me."

The very moment you commit your life to Jesus Christ, the truth of His Word instantly comes to pass in your spirit. Now that you're born again, there's a brand-new you!

Receive the Holy Spirit

As His child, your loving heavenly Father wants to give you the supernatural power you need to live a new life. "*For every one that asketh receiveth; and he that seeketh findeth; and to him that knocketh it shall be opened...how much more shall your heavenly Father give the Holy Spirit to them that ask him?*" (Luke 11:10–13 KJV).

All you have to do is ask, believe, and receive!

Pray this: "Father, I recognize my need for Your power to live a new life. Please fill me with Your Holy Spirit. By faith, I receive it right now. Thank You for baptizing me. Holy Spirit, You are welcome in my life."

Congratulations! Now you're filled with God's supernatural power.

Some syllables from a language you don't recognize will rise up from your heart to your mouth (1 Corinthians 14:14). As you speak them out loud by faith, you're releasing God's power from within and building yourself up in the spirit (1 Corinthians 14:4). You can do this whenever and wherever you like.

It doesn't really matter whether you felt anything or not when you prayed to receive the Lord and His Spirit. If you believed in your heart that you received, then God's Word promises you did. "*Therefore I say unto you, What things soever ye desire, when ye pray, believe that ye receive them, and ye shall have them*" (Mark 11:24 KJV). God always honors His Word—believe it!

Please contact me and let me know that you've prayed to receive Jesus as your Savior or be filled with the Holy Spirit. I would like to rejoice with you and help you understand more fully what has taken place in your life. I'll send you a free gift that will help you understand and grow in your new relationship with the Lord.

Welcome to your new life!

Call for Prayer

If you need prayer for any reason, you can call our Prayer Line 24 hours a day, seven days a week at 719-635-1111. A trained prayer minister will answer your call and pray with you. Every day, we receive testimonies of healings and other miracles from our Prayer Line, and we are ministering God's nearly-too-good-to-be-true message of the Gospel to more people than ever. So I encourage you to call today!

CONTACT INFORMATION

Charis Bible College

800 Gospel Truth Way

Woodland Park, CO 80863

info@charisbiblecollege.org

Helpline Available 24/7: 719-635-1111

CharisBibleCollege.org

Also visit Carrie at CarriePickett.com